DESIGNING PORNOTOPIA

DESIGNING PORNOTOPIA

Travels in Visual Culture

RICK POYNOR

PRINCETON ARCHSS, NEW YORK

Published in 2006 by
Princeton Architectural Press
37 East Seventh Street
New York, New York 10003

For a free catalog of books, call 1.800.722.6657.
Visit our website at www.papress.com.

This book was designed and produced in 2006 by
Laurence King Publishing Ltd., London
© 2006 Rick Poynor
The moral right of the author has been asserted.

Designed and typeset by Nick Bell design

Picture research by Andy Prince

For Princeton Architectual Press:
Project editor: Nicola Bednarek
Special thanks to: Nettie Aljian, Dorothy Ball,
Janet Behning, Becca Casbon, Penny (Yuen Pik)
Chu, Russell Fernandez, Peter Fitzgerald, Jan
Haux, Clare Jacobson, John King, Mark Lamster,
Nancy Eklund Later, Linda Lee, Katharine Myers,
Lauren Nelson, Scott Tennent, Jennifer Thompson,
Paul Wagner, Joseph Weston, and Deb Wood of
Princeton Architectural Press —Kevin C. Lippert,
publisher

Library of Congress Cataloging-in-Publication Data
Poynor, Rick.
   Designing pornotopia : essays on visual culture /
Rick Poynor.
      p. cm.
   Includes bibliographical references and index.
   ISBN-13: 978-1-56898-607-4 (alk. paper)
   ISBN-10: 1-56898-607-6 (alk. paper)
   1. Commercial art. 2. Graphic arts. 3. Sex in art.
I. Title.
   NC998.4.P68 2006
   741.609'0511—dc22
                              2006003607

Printed in China

Cover illustration: Ken Leung at Nick Bell design
Typography: Documenta ST Regular from Dutch
Type Library, Kada from Lineto, Klavika Bold from
Process Type Foundry

For Hilary

INTRODUCTION

In the summer of 2005, a branch of W.H. Smith in Croydon, south London, found itself the target of an unusual protest. A group of schoolgirls, aged 11 to 15, picketed the retailer because they objected to it selling Playboy-branded stationery aimed at teenage girls. These items included pencil cases, diaries, ring binders, gel pens and notepads emblazoned with Playboy's bow-tie-wearing bunny symbol, which has been identified for decades with the magazine that Hugh Hefner started in 1953. Bunny girls employed at Playboy Clubs around the world were notorious for their bunny-ear headbands, bow ties and fluffy white tails. A pressure group, Object, criticized W.H. Smith for its decision to stock the range, which is, according to the shop, one of the most popular it has ever sold. 'Playboy's logo clearly represents pornography,' noted Object. 'The magazine routinely features sexualised and full-frontal images of naked young women. It also promotes pornographic videos and strip shows ... W.H. Smith is therefore endorsing pornography to young, impressionable and possibly under-age girls."

W.H. Smith made light of this complaint. According to a spokes-woman, the product was just a fashion range, a harmless bit of fun, with no inappropriate imagery and no deeper significance. 'We offer customers choice,' said the company's head of media relations. 'We're not here to act as a moral censor.'[2] The shop could see no problem at all with displaying the pink Playboy products alongside other stationery ranges aimed at children, such as Bratz and Funky Friends. In Croydon, the schoolgirls' teacher accompanied them on their street protest. She reported that, until she explained the bunny's origins, many of the 11- and 12-year-olds had no idea that the cute logo represented the porn industry. Meanwhile, for older girls, the image of the glamour model, which Playboy epitomizes, is everywhere presented as a positive career choice.

The story seemed symptomatic of our times in a number of ways. First, because it involved something as elementary, on the face of it, as a piece of graphic design, a logo. For some observers, though seemingly only a minority, the symbol represents in concentrated graphic form an unacceptable set of assumptions about women's social and sexual roles. The use of the bunny in such an inappropriate place as children's school equipment shows how mainstream porn has become. For others, including W.H. Smith and many parents who buy their daughters items from the Playboy range, the logo appears to carry no adverse associations whatsoever. It is simply a cuddly rabbit, like a toy or pet, an appealing image that requires no further consideration. It is not as though the branding makes any overt allusions to posing naked for the enjoyment of male magazine readers and viewers of porn videos. Nevertheless, it is hard to view this as a healthy development. A logo linked for years with the objectification of women is being insinuated into the minds of young girls and made normal and respectable.

If a high-street retailer such as W.H. Smith is unable to see the problem, it can only be because the normalization of porn is now so advanced. The casting aside of inhibitions has been under way since the 1960s. It was given a boost by the arrival of home video and with the coming of the World Wide Web in the 1990s the urge to strip away the final shreds of decorum became unstoppable. In the last few years, sexual images have thrust their way into the everyday public sphere. One of the most telling instances of this change is the sexually explicit content of films such as *Romance* and *Anatomy of Hell* from France and *Intimacy* and *9 Songs* from Britain, which could never have been passed for public viewing in the UK a decade ago without substantial cuts.

Before 2000, it was unusual to see much acknowledgement of this growing sexual openness in mainstream design, but in the last few years designers have joined the party. The convergence of sex and design makes perfect sense. Both are compulsively visual and tactile;

both offer a realm of sensual pleasure and hedonism; both are treated as recreational activities; and both are viewed in openly self-preoccupied, consumerist terms. Contemporary design – a world of fab furniture, luxurious interiors, trendy graphics, fashionable restaurants, hip hotels and places to shop conceived as temples of sublime self-indulgence – provides a seamless backdrop for contemporary sex. In 2001, it was startling to see an article about the design of sex toys in the American industrial design magazine *I.D.* Yes, indeed, these gizmos must be conceived and designed by someone based on some kind of research before they can be manufactured and marketed, but politeness had previously drawn a veil over the details.[3] Before long, ultra-chic product designers such as Marc Newson and Tom Dixon were making well-publicized contributions to the cause of human happiness in the shape of sleek silicone and resin sex aids with names like Mojo and Bone. By 2005, there was nothing unseemly about finding a feature in *Design Week* rounding up the latest programmable, non-penetrative vibrator by industrial designer Geoff Hollington and the new Durex Play range of three-speed, rechargeable pleasure tools by Seymour Powell, better known until then for designing kettles, hair-dryers and toasters.[4]

Graphic design, too, was travelling fast up the same path. In 2003, in what must surely have been a first for a professional design magazine, *Grafik* published spreads from a book by fashion photographers David Bailey and Rankin featuring close-ups of female genitals as part of a special report on 'Seduction'. 'These are some of the most intimate images of the female body you are ever likely to see – unless you are a consumer of hardcore pornography, that is,' noted the article.[5] The book, a piece of unrestrained designer fetishism in its own right, came in a Perspex slipcase designed with impeccable taste by Mark Farrow, long-term collaborator with the Pet Shop Boys. In an editorial published a few issues later, *Grafik*'s editor mused amiably on the subject of porn consumption in the workplace, the contradictions in male attitudes to explicit pictures and the shortcomings of images of naked men created for viewers like herself.[6] It was a far cry from the usual design magazine editorial bromides about free pitching, the latest round of award winners and the pursuit of creative excellence.

Today, examples of the new sex-and-design sensibility can be found wherever you turn. An issue of *Colors* magazine on the theme of 'Lust' features a report on LA Couples, a Los Angeles nightclub where people take part in group sex. A double-page colour illustration is packed with duos and trios getting intimately acquainted on the mattresses while others look on.[7] The magazine, long noted for its design awareness, is aimed at young people, including teenagers, but the image contains nothing they will not have seen many times on the Internet and probably have done themselves. If that seems a little obvious, visit London's trendiest design book shop, Magma, to pick up a copy of *Dirty Found*, an offshoot of *Found* magazine, which collects bits of private writing, drawings and photos that readers have discovered lying around in the street and other public places and sent in for publication. Assembled like a scrapbook with graphic gusto and considerable humour, *Dirty Found* offers an unprecedented, un-retouched glimpse of the bodies, erotic fantasies and sexual pastimes of ordinary people, a pop culture version of the kind of intimate material that the Kinsey Institute for sex research in the US used to classify and archive behind closed doors. If your budget can stretch to an erotic photograph by Helmut Newton or Bob Carlos Clarke, or a black leather *chaise longue* with stirrups, then a new London gallery in Charing Cross Road has been created with your tastes in mind. 'Charing X is about art, design and ideas that challenge the boundaries of conventional sexual territories,' explain the gallery's founders, David Grob and Adae-Elena Amats, owner of the erotic shop Coco de Mer in Covent Garden, London.[8]

There is probably no need to go on. As this book's title suggests, we are in the process of designing a pornotopia in which sex, or at least our dreams of sex, are allowed to permeate areas of life they would never have been permitted to enter until recently. American literary critic Steven Marcus coined the word 'pornotopia' in his book *The Other Victorians*, published in 1966. Marcus's fascinating study analyzes the pornographic writing, hidden from the view of respectable society, which was privately published in mid-19th century Victorian England. This forbidden literature is notable for its obsessive exclusion of everything except for sexual activity, presenting a kind of utopia based on nothing other than doing it. Utopia is by definition a 'not place' or 'not a place' – it does not and cannot exist. Pornotopia, writes Marcus, is 'that vision which regards all of human experience as a series of exclusively sexual events or conveniences'.[9] Elsewhere, he adds that pornotopia is 'the imagination of the entire universe beneath the sign of sexuality'.[10] Marcus was writing at a transitional moment in the development of pornography. His concern was with words rather than imagery and it was by then possible to publish these novels and other pornographic texts legally. Marcus recognized that huge social changes were under way and he was inclined to see these positively, though he noted their limitations: 'We have in our own time been witness to a sexual revolution which has also been split off from what might have been expected to accompany it – impulses of a social revolutionary kind."[11] This insight has proved to be entirely correct, though Marcus's hope that our society might be about to outgrow its preoccupation with pornography was clearly over-optimistic.

I am using 'pornotopia' here in a wider, more social, less literary sense than Marcus. What he could not have predicted in the 1960s, with his focus on the past, was how technology would soon make pornographic images available to anyone at any time. Marcus says he would be troubled if he saw his young son reading a copy of De Sade's *Justine*, but the French libertine's writing is hardly a concern today. A 200-year-old novel easily overlooked by most people pales beside the influence of a global media culture that has so inured us to porn that Playboy logos on pencil cases seem normal to many.

As a collection of essays, *Designing Pornotopia* does not set out to offer a single, unified argument. Like its predecessor *Obey the Giant*, it is a set of interlinked observations and reflections on contemporary visual culture intended to question and provoke. Pornotopia can perhaps be viewed in a more general sense as a metaphor for a system of relations between people and for the way we see ourselves and each other. Many of these essays focus on the body as a vulnerable personal space where social pressures and impulses converge and inscribe their imperatives. Pornography wants us to think of ourselves only as bodies. Ordinary people, influenced by images of perfection seen in glossy magazines and porn, seek to enhance bodies they regard as inadequate by means of plastic surgery. Artists fantasize about remaking the body prosthetically and scientists speculate about redesigning it genetically. Designers such as Stefan Sagmeister and Elliott Earls employ their bodies as another kind of graphic surface, while illustrator Paul Davis visualizes the body as an expression of inner disturbance. J.G. Ballard conjectures a world not far from our own where out-of-control bodies and technology slam together in a destructive union of metal and flesh.

My view of the changes documented here is often critical, but caught in the thick of them with everyone else I make no claim to have all the answers. Some developments that I find to be matters for concern appear to leave others untroubled. That in itself gives pause for doubt. Whatever misgivings we might harbour about the direction and pace of social change, only time will tell whether people find a positive way to assimilate or overcome these trends, or whether things will turn out for the worse, though the signs are not encouraging. As our vocabulary reshapes itself to reflect new preoccupations and styles of living, earlier ways of understanding and criticizing social reality regarded by many as no longer relevant can fall into disuse and disappear. Cultural critic Judith Williamson notes this with reference to the feminist critique of sexism: 'sexism isn't just a phenomenon, it's an idea – and once the word stops being used, the idea goes out of fashion.'[12] Objections to the Playboy logo and to the imagery described in the title essay, 'Designing Pornotopia', make perfect sense to people familiar with feminist thinking. Without these tools, we lack the basic concepts to analyze these images and to formulate a critical response.

Maybe what we see here is that the market has already decided how the future will be – if we are willing to let it happen.

HYPHENATION NATION

Early in the 1990s, I was contacted by a Japanese magazine seeking nominations from design people for a word or concept that would, according to their crystal balls, 'define the coming decade'. My suggestion was *hybrid*. What a frisson that word then seemed to produce! It suggested a cultural landscape in which old categories of design artificially – and boringly – held apart by outmoded convention would merge in productive and exciting new forms. It contained more than a hint of transgression, as worn-out ways of thinking, making and acting gave way to liberating creative practices, ideas and experiences. I was thinking about the old dividing line between art and design, often questioned for sure, but in most real institutional situations still firmly in place. The drive to blur it all seemed everywhere apparent, and postmodernism, still much talked about then, actively encouraged blurring as part of the ongoing meltdown of 'high' and 'low'.

A decade later, the idea of hybridity is now deeply entrenched in the design world. Both the idea and, to some extent, the activity have become commonplace, although that doesn't stop designers from enthusing about hybridization as though it were the freshly cut key to a whole new cultural kingdom. In his heavily promoted book *Life Style*, Bruce Mau, Toronto-based graphic designer and sometime collaborator with Rem Koolhaas, rehearses a view of hybridity that few of his

Prada shop, New York, 2001. Interior architecture: OMA. Wallpaper design: 2x4.

designer readers would be inclined to dispute: 'Attempting to declare the discrete boundary of any practice, where one ends and another begins, has become arbitrary and artificial,' he writes. 'On the contrary, the overlap is where the greatest innovation is happening.'[1] The two examples that follow this assertion are oddly lightweight, to say the least. Mau mentions the intersection of cinema and digital manipulation seen in Gap commercials and *The Matrix*'s action sequences. These media forms are neither one thing nor the other, he proposes, but 'a monstrous and beautiful child of the two'.[2] Then, to represent the birth of a new kind of culture, Mau jumps to an image adapted from Nietzsche of a chorus in which every singer is a soloist, pushing forward to outsing the others, pressing against the audience and surrounding them so that they are 'embedded' in this singing mass. It is impossible to tell from this passage whether Mau regards this condition as desirable or undesirable, enabling or disabling. Are we, for some reason, supposed to welcome what appears to be an oppressive restriction of our own free movement?

 Whether we are talking about image technology, global markets or digital infrastructure, Mau continues, all of these things demand a 'predatory colonization of open space'.[3] We have reached the point, he explains, where 'Spheres once thought free [from the logic of the market], and even resistant or opposed to it – the museum, the academy, public democratic space – find it ever more difficult to retain autonomy in the face of corporate culture and its sponsorships, educational initiatives, and so-called civic gestures.'[4] As small-scale examples of this intrusion, Mau cites print ads above urinals and video ads in elevators, and rightly says these represent just the beginning of a process of 'inscription' by commercial imperatives to which there is potentially no end. In the space of just a few hundred words, Mau has moved from an excited declaration that hybridity and the dissolution of boundaries are generating our most significant cultural innovations to an almost neutral-sounding acknowledgement that practically nowhere, apart from a few unspoiled bits of nature, is free from 'hostile takeover' by market forces. The direction of his argument implies a link between the two, but he doesn't acknowledge it outright and this reluctance to make and act on the connection is symptomatic of the bind in which many designers now find themselves.

The market itself shows no such hesitation to engineer and exploit the link. Business literature provides an abundance of evidence that cultural ideas that might have seemed avant-garde and progressive in artistic circles 10 or 15 years ago are now routine shop talk in business circles. *Funky Business* by Jonas Ridderstråle and Kjell Nordström, a pair of Swedish PhDs who brandish their hairless heads as a hip personal trademark, is an international best-seller translated, at last count, into 21 languages. King of the corporate gurus Tom Peters, for one, thinks they offer a 'defiantly funky perspective on the new world order', and this new world order is founded on the twin principles, interminably reiterated, of continuous change and exhilarating uncertainty. According to Ridderstråle and Nordström, we live in a 'blurred society' in which conventional divisions and structures, once used to sort experience into neat categories, are falling into a state of disarray: industries and relationships between companies are blurring, products and services are blurring, and so is the traditional distinction between leisure and work. 'Everywhere we look, we see blur – East-West, Men-Women, Structure-Process, Right-Wrong.'[5] For entrepreneurial individuals and organizations, they argue, these changes are not mysterious or threatening and they don't spell chaos; they should instead be grasped as opportunities to restructure and innovate.

The funky Swedes offer a vision of the future in which we inhabit a cut-and-paste 'hyphe-nation' where the solution to having more than enough of what already exists is to create a never-ending stream of brand-new things by combining old things in novel ways – 'the weirder the combination,' they exult, 'the more unique the result'.[6] They list some recent hyphenations: edu-tainment, info-tainment, distance-learning, psycho-linguistics, bio-tech, corporate-university. As they see it, variation has the potential to breed ever more variation as gleaming new hyphenates are deliriously spliced together in a chain of multiplication that is potentially limitless, so long as value is added in the process. 'At the same time,' they caution, 'it needs to be difficult for the consumer to unbundle the offering. Because if the customer can easily separate the things that have been combined, he or she can use increasingly perfected markets to get one or all of these items from someone else.'[7]

While it was doubtless not their intention, Ridderstråle and Nordström have succinctly expressed the problem faced by many cultural producers today and, perhaps above all, by designers. The question is precisely how it might be possible to 'unbundle the offering'. In the relationship of business and culture, the process of blurring, hyphenation, hybridization – call it what you will – is so far advanced that it is easy to take it for granted and cease to question what might have been lost on the way. All the rhetoric focuses relentlessly on what is supposedly gained. Merely to use the word 'innovation' as a rallying cry, as Mau does, as the business-friendly Swedes do, is to suggest developments that cannot be gainsaid, wealth-generating outcomes that, according to the logic of the market, are inherently desirable, irrespective of their ulterior meanings or effects.

By the end of the 1990s, the feeling that there was almost no resisting these changes ran deep and, this being the case, the only sensible response was to collude. In December 1999, an issue of *Utne Reader* with the cover story 'The Great American Sellout' noted: 'The rewards are now so high it's often seen as foolish, even pathological, to resist.'[8] A British novelist, writing in the style magazine *Dazed & Confused*, set out the new priorities for herself and her friends: 'Fuck all that spiritual bullshit about mental growth and exploration and experience, we wanted the goods. The hardware. Cash, clothes, cars, luxury apartments.'[9] A London design journalist, Alice Rawsthorn, now director of the city's Design Museum, phrased the issue more delicately, though just as materialistically, in promotional copy for the fashion company Caterpillar. It took eight years, she notes, between Jack Kerouac setting off on the road and his appearance in *Playboy*'s 'Beat' issue, while hot artist Tracey Emin made it on to billboards for Bombay Sapphire gin in a matter of months and was handsomely recompensed for it. 'Maybe the commercialisation thing we get so hung up on these days comes down to just that,' Rawsthorn offers. 'If everything's now up for grabs, then are you master or servant of your own life's commodification?'[10]

In 2001, the style magazine *Sleazenation* provided one possible answer with what some might have regarded as a truly innovative cover concept – 'Absolut(e) sell out'. On the back cover, it ran an Absolut ad, 'Absolut Morph' (the new product blends vodka and citrus flavours; hyphenation and mutability are, once again, the visual theme), while the front showed a model sporting covetable items by Yves Saint Laurent, Gucci and Chanel, with prices and supplier details attached. 'To a certain extent we are all sell-outs now,' the editor confessed in a note. 'Any individual or organisation attempting to disseminate their cultural message will find that corporate involvement – i.e. cash – is becoming increasingly necessary to facilitate this. This is not necessarily a good thing or a bad thing. It is also inevitable.'[11] No argument about its inevitability from the business side: an issue of *Fast Company* proposed that fringe ideas generated by artistic deviants are the stuff of mass markets. The magazine's advice? 'Sell out! Sure, it lacks integrity, but the benefits can be pretty nice.'[12]

Once we dissolve the old boundary lines and concede the territory to corporate forces, it is extremely difficult to win it back. From our compromised position embedded in the new hyphenated reality, in which the culture-business depends on the drip-drip-drip of corporate largesse, it becomes hard to imagine that there could be any other way of doing things, especially if this is the only reality we have known. Any misgivings can be waved aside with the claim that this state of affairs is now simply inevitable, so we might as well grab the benefits with both hands, and any criticism can be rejected as a point of view that naively fails to understand the financial expediency of culture's pact with commerce. When Morgan Stanley, sponsor of 'Surrealism: Desire Unbound' at Tate Modern in London, draws a parallel between the way the Surrealists 'threw back the boundaries of conventional art by challenging conventional thinking' and its own history of 'challenging traditional thinking to help our clients raise their financial aspirations', such a comparison has long since ceased to strike some of us as the slightest bit absurd.[13]

In a fascinating polemic, *The Twilight of American Culture*, social critic Morris Berman takes a scathing look at the US today and concludes that, despite the vigour and vitality of contemporary commercial culture, the nation is locked into a pattern of decline – evinced by social inequality, loss of entitlements, decreasing intellectual abilities and spiritual death – which it is powerless to prevent. This decline will play itself out regardless and the outcome will not be known until we are no longer around. What can be done then, here and now, to ensure that, when the time finally comes, enlightened values still survive so that a more receptive society can make use of them again to revivify itself? Berman's answer is a strategy inspired by what happened to classical knowledge during the Dark Ages when the manuscripts were faithfully copied and preserved in the monasteries by monks who almost certainly did not understand their contents. When the moment for cultural revival came in the twelfth century, the knowledge was there to be used. Berman calls his proposal 'the monastic option' and the essence of the idea is that people who don't feel they fit in with consumer society's prevailing values find ways of practising at a local level – and so keeping alive – the values they hold dear. He stresses the individualistic nature of this strategy, cautions against the constant dangers of institutionalization and co-optation by commerce, and rejects the notion of a life based on kitsch, consumerism, profit, fame and self-promotion. Among his examples are *Adbusters*, David Barsamian's 'Alternative Radio' programme on National Public Radio and violinist Olga Bloom's Bargemusic, which presents chamber music in a wood-panelled concert hall in a converted coffee barge floating off Brooklyn. Berman accepts the fact that we have no way of knowing how the future will turn out and that his idea might be no more than wishful thinking. Yet, as he reasonably observes, 'If we make *no* attempt to preserve the best in our culture, we can rest assured that the possibility of cultural renewal is pretty much ruled out.'[14]

Even if they agree with this conclusion, most designers will probably wish to find a way of collaborating with commercial forces. They frequently talk about 'changing things from the inside', but to do this, if it is possible at all, will require a clarity of political analysis, a strength of critical purpose and a tactical readiness to accept the fact that most interventions are likely to be short-lived, while the fundamental nature of the political and economic system remains intact. Few seem to possess these tools in practice and even those who come closest have drawn legitimate criticism. The late Tibor Kalman, starting from the premise that 'Our culture is corporate culture', proposes a 'modest solution' in his book *Perverse Optimist*: 'Find the cracks in the wall.' In other words, hook up with entrepreneurs crazy enough to allow you to use their money to change the world.[15] Kalman's most sustained attempt to do this was with Benetton, for whom he conceived and edited 13 issues of *Colors* magazine. Thomas Frank, writing in *Artforum*, was perhaps the only commentator to point out the naivety of Kalman's political position, which posed no fundamental challenge to the knitwear giant.[16] In *Life Style*, Mau's opening gambit is to distance himself from culture jammers (such as *Adbusters*, presumably) who do at least make it clear where they stand with their anti-corporate rhetoric and actions. Mau's definition of engagement with the conditions of our time, or what he calls the 'global image economy', apparently requires that judgement be postponed 'while we search for an exit'.[17] If this sounds unhelpfully hazy, much of what Mau has to say in the book about his practice seems simultaneously oracular and opaque, a warning sign that he wants to have it both ways, to reap the professional rewards of working for the 'regime of the logo and its image' (Mau's words) while affecting to critique it – a contradiction pointed out in reviews by both Mark Kingwell and Hal Foster.[18]

One senses here the influence of Mau's colleague Rem Koolhaas, an architect and observer for whom the suspension of judgement has become an operational strategy. The problem, as always, is how to 'unbundle the offering' as these culture-business hybrids become increasingly imaginative, persuasive and compelling. Dan Weiden, founder and CEO of Weiden+Kennedy, Nike's advertising agency for the last 20 years, renovated a 90-year-old landmark building in Portland's downtown Pearl District. Then, in a canny move, he invited the Portland Institute of Contemporary Art (PICA), a fledgling arts organization with a reputation for promoting edgy young artists, to become a tenant. Weiden was already a PICA board member, and he hoped that the presence of artists would help re-energize the agency's creative atmosphere by blurring the boundaries imposed by traditional conceptions of advertising and by opening up fresh ways of communicating.

'It's not altruism – it's an investment,' he told *Fast Company*. 'And in some ways, it's extremely selfish. The bet is that there will be concrete rewards and spiritual rewards for us and for our clients, who hire us to talk to people in a way that's both meaningful and surprising.'[19] It is easy to see the appeal for a struggling arts institution of finding a home in such a spectacular space (designed by Brad Cloepfil and his firm Allied Works Architecture), just as it takes no great leap of imagination to grasp what a pleasure it would be for agency personnel to work in such an ambience. Yet the relationship is troubling because it crystallizes a systemic truth about the relative power of advertising and a local arts organization, as the larger of the two entities literally ingests and displays the smaller, weaker one for its own purposes. The implication for both advertising and art, and for people in the community who visit PICA in this space, is that the boundaries are now fully permeable and that art and advertising are not so different in essence – it is all just 'creativity' and 'communication'. The process of boundary-erosion is happening everywhere and PICA's presence within W+K only confirms its normality.

At Prada's 'Epicenter' store on Prince Street and Broadway in Manhattan, this erosion is even more subtly embodied. The hybridization of culture and commerce has been so artfully achieved here that, walking around the 2,276-square metre (24,500-square-foot) space designed by Rem Koolhaas and OMA, one doesn't experience the queasy sensation of being an interloper that snooty fashion shops so often induce. The underlying sales function is giddily subsumed into something much more loosely defined. With its half-hidden video screens in all shapes and sizes, its huge cylindrical glass-sided elevator and its vast wallpapered wall, it is more like the latest thing in funky, high-tech arts centres than a shop. If the Italian fashion company means to convey the impression that its Epicenter store is, at least in part, a public space, then it succeeds; on Saturdays the place is reportedly thronged by people who have dropped by to hang out and gawk.

Prada planned to stage public performances in the auditorium sculpted from a ravishing sweep of zebrawood.

'In a world where everything is shopping … and shopping is everything … what is luxury?' asks Koolhaas in a Prada book about the project that is as thick as a telephone directory. 'Luxury is NOT shopping.' The book defines luxury in four ways: as intelligence; as attention – once captured, this is generously 'handed back' to the consumer; as roughness – an antidote to the unremitting smoothness of the commercial realm; and as waste – 'Space that is not "productive" – not shopping – affords contemplation, privacy, mobility, and luxury'. Then, a few pages later, under the heading of 'Street', there is a mysterious hint about eventually returning 'the public back to the public …'[20]

This and other statements by Koolhaas, along with Mau's attempt to locate the exit, suggest that we shall one day emerge from the hyphenation nation. How it will happen, they don't say. How projects that serve commercial efforts are going to bring it about, they also don't say. Maybe the time has come to insist on the validity of some of our earlier categories and distinctions – between art and non-art, between instrumental work and work undertaken for its own sake. Operating without them is about as effective, as a method of resistance, as looking for a pathway in a fog.

MEET ME AT THE CHECKOUT

It is not easy to imagine Rem Koolhaas going shopping. The tall, lean Dutchman, one of the few genuine superstars of contemporary architecture, a man able to pack lecture theatres with rapt admirers wherever he speaks, looks much too cerebral and abstemious to relish an afternoon at the mall. Yet for Koolhaas, initiating a huge research project into the future of the city at Harvard University, shopping showed every sign of being 'the final human programme', the destination we have been struggling to reach all along. 'I had a sense that if you looked at this issue carefully you would be able to decipher to what terminal point our cities seem to be evolving,' he says.

The outcome of Koolhaas's survey, conducted with a team of Harvard postgraduates, is published by Taschen, best known for inexpensive art books and cheerfully unembarrassed erotica. It is typical of Koolhaas's wish to challenge and provoke that the 800-page, fully annotated and footnoted *Harvard Design School Guide to Shopping* is being handled by one of the most commercially aggressive coffee-table book publishers, rather than a staid university press.[1] It is accompanied by *Great Leap Forward*, an equally monumental volume by Koolhaas and his students about the phenomenal rate of urban development in China's Pearl River Delta – another sign of cities to come, argues Koolhaas, whether his fellow architects like it or not.[2]

As an architect, Koolhaas cultivates an ambiguous stance. He came to architecture late, at the age of 25, after starting his career as a journalist, then writing screenplays, and regards himself as equal parts writer and architect. 'I am still sceptical and therefore unwilling to completely identify with the profession,' he once remarked. Even so, projects such as the Netherlands Dance Theatre in The Hague (1987), the Kunsthal art gallery in Rotterdam (1992) and his urban master plan for the Euralille high-speed train hub in France (1994) are hugely influential. Koolhaas's residence in Bordeaux for a paralysed publisher, completed in 1998, is already regarded as a canonical modern house. Its astonishing centrepiece, the owner's study, doubles as a room-sized lift able to move between wine cellar, library and bedroom. Koolhaas rejects conventional ideas of beauty and order, favouring brutal collisions of detail and surface and the appearance of instability and flux. One eminent American architecture critic hailed him as 'the Le Corbusier of our times'. In 2000, he was the first Dutch architect to be awarded the Pritzker Prize, architecture's equivalent of the Nobel.

Books, just as much as buildings, have been central to Koolhaas's rise as an architect and, on past evidence, the Taschen titles will make waves. He came to fame with a book, *Delirious New York* (1978), a turbocharged manifesto and polemic in which he visualizes high-rise Manhattan as a laboratory for a new lifestyle – 'the culture of congestion'. The surreal cover shows the Empire State Building and the Chrysler Building lying in bed together in a state of post-coital bliss. In 1995, Koolhaas and the Canadian graphic designer Bruce Mau published S,M,L,XL, a 1,300-page, silver-clad labyrinth of writing by Koolhaas and projects by his studio, the Office for Metropolitan Architecture (OMA). *Time* magazine called it 'the ultimate coffee-table book for a generation raised by both MTV and Derrida' and it became a best-selling cult book.

OMA's controversial design for the Seattle Central Library opened in 2004, two new galleries for the ever-expanding Guggenheim Museum and the Hermitage have opened in Las Vegas, and Koolhaas's visionary proposal to relocate Schiphol Airport to a man-made island in the North Sea could be given the go-ahead at any time. ('It's inevitable,' he insists.) He spends one week out of every three criss-crossing the globe, but prefers to maintain his base in Rotterdam, where he was born. 'It's a city without a scene and a city without distractions,' he says. 'You can be utterly focused and utterly anonymous.'

OMA occupies the seventh floor of a bland, grey office block on the edge of a residential district not far from the central station. At any one time, Koolhaas employs between 60 and 80 architects in Rotterdam; a further 20 are based in New York, close to Canal Street in SoHo. We talk in Koolhaas's office, in which designer trappings are kept to a minimum. There is a classic black Anglepoise lamp on his desk and an open box of 50 red Bic pens, suggesting stern corrective tendencies. A postcard on display says, 'Money creates taste'.

Koolhaas wears a white, short-sleeved cotton shirt, grey trousers with perfect creases and black, elastic-sided boots. He speaks in a low, almost unassuming monotone, rarely raising his voice. He wants to know whether I have seen *Great Leap Forward* and within moments he has piled the desk with dummies for the Chinese book and for two other Harvard research projects – about Lagos and the Roman Empire as a model of globalization – as well as a dummy for a book about Communism. He transmits an immediate impression of daunting productivity and energy. He is generous with his attention, yet at the same time preoccupied. It takes him some time to settle and our interview is punctuated by phone calls, and interruptions from his assistant who explodes through a side door.

Koolhaas is uncomfortable with the suggestion that he is a fashionable figure and he 'systematically refuses' invitations to appear as a talking head on Dutch TV. Nor will he discuss his feelings about the guru-like standing he enjoys among architects who flock to hear his predictions, buy his books and imitate his work. 'I have no comment, basically. It's really not healthy for me to speculate on it.' For the young architects who work with him, the experience appears to be both inspiring and exhausting. One tells me wearily that he is brilliant, though demanding and tough.

In 1995, when Koolhaas was appointed professor of architecture and urban design at Harvard, he made his terms clear from the start. 'I became a teacher there on condition that I had no involvement whatsoever with design,' he says. Harvard gives him a free hand. He recognized that in an age of globalization the student body represents an unusual repository of professional and cultural knowledge, and this inspired the idea of researching 'moments of drastic change' in the city. For the Chinese field trips, more than half of the students spoke Chinese. The shopping project has researchers from Britain, the US, Japan, China, Korea, Singapore, Yugoslavia and the Canary Islands.

'I was totally exhausted by the completely redundant way in which the idea of the city is talked about,' says Koolhaas. 'I think our entire vocabulary is useless: "public space", "public realm" … all these things have been completely transformed and so what we are trying to do is reinvent ways of talking about the city.' The only way to modernize architecture, he suggests, is to take seriously the extent to which it has been undermined by contemporary commercial and political developments, and then to see whether there are new ways of redefining architecture so that, instead of passively suffering these changes, we can exploit them. He believes that classical ideas about the organization of the city, of the kind espoused by Richard Rogers and Norman Foster, attempt to reassert values that are simply not institutionally, economically or politically imaginable any more. According to Koolhaas, the street is dead and the rise of the 'generic city' liberated from old ideas about the need for a centre and a unique identity – seen above all in the Far East – signals the demise of urban planning ('planning makes no difference whatsoever'). Just about the only activity left is shopping.

Koolhaas and his team have the figures to prove it. They estimate that there are almost 2 billion square metres (21.5 billion square feet) of retail space in the world. Thirty-nine per cent of this is in the US, 37 per cent in Asia and 10 per cent in Europe (Africa lays claim to just 0.3 per cent of the world's total retail space). In the *Guide to Shopping*, this space is dramatically visualized as a factor of Manhattan land surface area: the US has 12.7 Manhattans' worth of shopping space, Asia 12.1 and Europe a comparatively modest three. Wal-Mart, at 1.2 Manhattans, is the world's largest retailer. Its sales exceed the gross domestic product of three-quarters of the world's economies.

However, it is not simply that a vast amount of urban space is dedicated to retail activity. Shopping has a way of 'melting into everything', as the *Guide* puts it, and everything is 'melting into shopping'. Stations look like malls, airports look like malls and, in the US, even churches are pushing aside pews and altars in favour of mall-like food kiosks. Shopping has become increasingly central to museums and the rewards can be huge. The average American mall achieves sales of $250 per square foot. The Museum of Modern Art store in New York boasts sales of $1,750 per square foot. Airports, reconceived as shopping opportunities, produce spectacular profits. BAA, which owns seven UK airports, generates about 50 per cent of its income from its shops. In 2000, the group saw international revenues of £2.23 billion, of which £1.12 billion came from retail. Airport development is now synonymous with shopping.

Privatization has changed everything. 'The civic and social structures that guaranteed the continued existence of institutions such as museums, airports, churches, schools, and even the city have slowly

Drawing of a shopping mall, Jerde Partnership International

been dismantled,' notes Sze Tsung Leong, one of Koolhaas's co-editors. 'With governments no longer able or willing to support these institutions, financial support has shifted from a public to a private responsibility.... As much as we may deny or refuse it, shopping has become one of the only means by which we experience public life.'[3]

Quite how Koolhaas views these developments is not always clear. It is obvious that he enjoys needling other architects by confronting them with the unthinkable – architecture, he declares, has 'disappeared' – but he refrains from critical judgement, preferring the role of neutral observer. 'Judgements make you very heavy,' he says. 'It's like a mountaineer who has to travel light to get somewhere.' American critic Jeffrey Kipnis argues that while Koolhaas's work never overtly resists authority, 'it sabotages authority from within'. Others question Koolhaas's seeming neutrality. 'It must be hard being Rem,' says the architectural historian Charles Jencks. 'He knows what's going on. He has a heart. But he decided to put that on ice.'

Does Koolhaas enjoy shopping? He seems taken aback by the directness of the question. Like other theoretically inclined architects, he is happier discussing these issues in abstract terms. 'Well, of course, I'm a very urban person,' he says, 'and I have always been an urban person. I think what is important in terms of my general outlook is that I spent the years from 8 to 12 not in Europe but in Indonesia, after it had become independent. That is a situation where the entire city is a market and, of course, that is an incredibly exciting and mysterious condition, especially when you are young.' Back in Europe, he got rather less pleasure from the arrival of the shopping centre and these days he is more inclined towards research than participation.

In a coruscating essay in the *Guide to Shopping*, Koolhaas finally breaks cover and unveils a nightmarish vision, describing how a new kind of ugly, monotonous urban space, which he calls 'junkspace', is devouring cities and confusing once separate activities and forms of experience, turning our living spaces into textureless, characterless black holes. His words erupt in a scorching, unstoppable lava of insights and impressions. Junkspace, he writes, 'makes you uncertain where you are, obscures where you go, undoes where you were. Who do you think you are? Who do you want to be?'[4] This 'canned euphoria' is political in origin, he argues, both promiscuous and repressive, authorless yet surprisingly authoritarian, dependent, above all, on the 'removal of the critical faculty in the name of comfort and pleasure'.[5]

For a man who prefers not to judge, it is an unexpectedly critical statement of where he stands. But when I ask Koolhaas about it, his reply is as even-toned and measured as ever. 'I am basically optimistic that we are living in a system that in the end is capable of generating extreme intelligence,' he says. 'There is no doubt about that. This situation, which has got slightly out of hand, will somehow be, not so much corrected, but followed by something that finds new forms of interest.'

He cannot resist, however, adding a few ambiguous final remarks. Don't take the 'junkspace' tirade too seriously, he cautions. 'I decided to write in different genres. So this is the genre of "emotion" or "heart". No, no, I don't qualify it. I mean every word of it, but at the same time it was also an experiment on my part: OK, if they don't believe I have a heart, I'll show them I have a heart. It's amazing because people really are so happy that I have a heart. I find it so silly.'

LUXURIOUS FRUGALITY

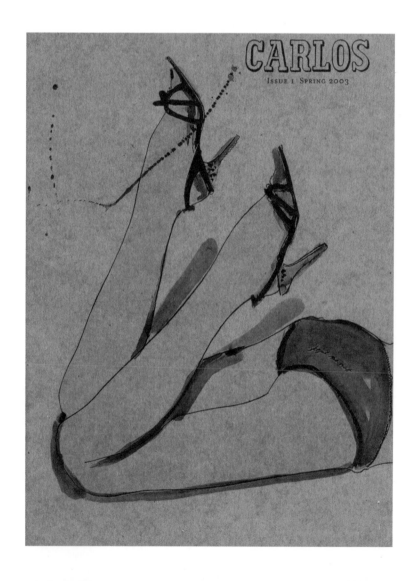

Carlos, no. 1, 2003.
Creative director: Jeremy
Leslie. Illustration:
Jonathan Schofield

Bourgeois bohemians began their inexorable ascent in the 1960s, so maybe it is fitting that Virgin Atlantic's in-flight magazine, aimed at its Upper Class passengers, is called *Carlos*. It is such a late 1960s/early 1970s kind of name: Carlos Santana, Carlos Castaneda, Carlos the Jackal (though terrorist associations may be less helpful here).

The magazine is certainly a 100 per cent bourgeois bohemian artefact. It will be read by people who American writer David Brooks, author of *Bobos in Paradise* (a 'bobo' is a bourgeois bohemian), describes, using the same words as Virgin, as 'the new upper class'. Bourgeois bohemians and the companies they work for – or own – have a lot of money, but they identify with anti-Establishment, countercultural styles rather than with the old, wealthy, ruling class. It is in their interest to have it both ways. 'The grand achievement of the educated elites in the 1990s was to create a way of living that lets you be an affluent success and at the same time a free-spirit rebel,' observes Brooks.[1]

In-flight magazines occupy a funny position in the publishing firmament. Anyone with a serious desire to read will have brought along books and magazines of their own. The slightly battered reading matter in the seat-back is for flipping through in idle moments, waiting to take off or land. Some airline magazines are admittedly well written and slickly designed, but it is hard to imagine casual browsers developing much of a loyalty. In-flight titles tend to follow dull news-stand conventions down to every last glossy detail.

Carlos, by contrast, rewrites the flight manual. The modest quarterly (measuring 170 x 240 millimetres/6 1/2 x 9 1/2 inches) looks like one of those slim Muji notebooks with a brown card cover. For bourgeois bohemians, as Brooks has noted, roughness signifies authenticity and virtue. In an image world that delivers photographs of hallucinatory brightness and intensity at every turn, luxury is conveyed by the absence of photos. The only photographs in *Carlos* come in an eight-page Paul Smith insert by Aboud Sodano, which looks more like an art project than advertising, as the designers probably planned.

The editorial pages, art directed by Warren Jackson for John Brown Citrus Publishing, which developed the magazine with Virgin Atlantic, have an informal, not-trying-too-hard kind of elegance – *McSweeny's* is a close cousin. All the type is printed dark blue on creamy, uncoated paper. The upper-case article intros, set in Mrs Eaves, waver eccentrically, though the columns, set in Hoefler Text, hold firm. Line drawings, another sure-fire sign of authenticity, feature throughout. They are often a bit artless, as in a portrait of Cameron Diaz for a drool-fest by film writer Joe Queenan. Doodles appear in the margins and sometimes drift into the text, but never to the point of distraction.

The visual mood might be quirky, even a touch enigmatic, but the content seems designed to relax and reassure. On the basis of the first issue, *Carlos* appears to assume that Upper Class flyers are fascinated by film, fashion and magazine publishing (which accounts for two articles). A passenger contributes an amusing list of bizarre things he has overheard said to the monkey in his laboratory. Acclaimed novelist Michel Faber writes a snooty short story about being caught in a lift with a bore. Ever wondered what Beck plays on his iPod? Well, now we know. There is a silly report on Gorgeous Networks, a dating and networking service for good-looking, successful people. One suspects that the reason for drawing this to the attention of Upper Class passengers is not entirely ironic.

There are few consumer experiences that dramatize inequality as vividly as air travel. A flexible ticket in Upper Class, flying from London to New York, costs ten times more than an economy seat. While most passengers wait grimly for the ordeal to end in battery-hen conditions of questionable safety, Upper Class travellers frequent their on-board bar, book massages with the beauty therapist and stretch out in cosy sleepsuits in 1.8 metres (6 feet) of sleeping space. *Carlos*, like so many products aimed at the deceptively frugal new upper class of bourgeois bohemians, is a smart idea, winningly executed. There is no obvious reason, in this case, why it could not be made available to anyone on the plane who wanted a copy. Or does Virgin believe that only the wealthy have the taste to appreciate it? As ever, culture is used as a way of bestowing privilege and drawing the boundary lines between different classes. Not so bohemian, when you think about it.

THIS MONTH'S COVER

One day, as we sometimes tell ourselves, paper will run out and we will have to rely entirely on our electronic networks to communicate, but until that day arrives we show no sign of abandoning our addiction to magazines. For sheer concentration of imagery in one place, there is no experience quite like going into a shop with a large selection of titles. At first sight your eye is overwhelmed by hundreds of shiny, brightly coloured rectangles, each one vibrating with pictures and lines of type. In a consumer society, we inhabit a ceaseless flow of images, coming at us at all times and from all directions, but nothing else has quite this degree of simultaneity: a field of competing attractions, in which all elements are equally present and vivid. Television and film, by contrast, present a flow of images in time; each new image erases and replaces the last. Our experience of the Internet is also sequential. Billboards have a commanding environmental presence, but a billboard is comparatively wasteful, using a lot of space to express a simple message. The same surface area, in a newsagent, book shop or supermarket display of magazines, fires out a vast multiplicity of signals.

There are other significant differences between our experience of magazine covers and other kinds of media. In order to engage with the magazine image-bank and peruse what it has to offer, you must approach it, enter its space, reach out and pick up its offerings. You move along the display racks, scanning each cover in turn, mingling with other people doing the same thing. Having picked up a magazine, you thumb through it and perhaps start to read. Dissatisfied, you replace one title and pick up another. If you are looking for a different type of magazine, you will have to move to another display. In a big shop, the sections will almost certainly be labelled to make it easier: music and hi-fi, current affairs, homes and gardens, sport. Another difference between magazines and other kinds of image consumption is that there is a direct causal link between seeing and buying. Cover images entice you, seduce you and you can possess them now and take them away to consume at leisure. In many respects, this is much like any other kind of shopping experience, especially browsing through CD covers in a record shop, or looking for books in a book shop. Books are comparable forms of visual and textual communication, but they lack magazines' intensity, urgency and promise of immediate gratification. A book addresses a defined subject, while a magazine covers a great range of topical subjects in less depth. Its lifespan is much shorter – a week, a month – and it clamours for attention now.

Clearly, there are also differences between the covers of magazines. A yachting monthly could never be confused with a computer monthly, but within a given category the distinction is much less marked. Computer magazines tend to look like other computer magazines and this is also true for each particular title. This month's cover looks slightly different from last month's cover – the reader has to perceive it as new – but not so different that the title no longer resembles itself. The feeling you have of almost limitless variety when you walk into a shop selling magazines is illusory. A degree of uniformity and predictability in content has become the very essence of the contemporary magazine and this is signalled to the reader by the conventions that govern its use of imagery and its cover design. These conventions are determined by marketing departments whose task is to sell the maximum number of copies, with the paradoxical result that a magazine's most loyal and committed readers are simply taken for granted. 'The problem with covers is you end up trying to catch the floating readers,' notes Robin Derrick, art director of British *Vogue*. 'You ignore the 100,000 who buy the magazine every month and target the 200,000 who occasionally buy it.'[1]

It has been marketing wisdom for many years that, especially when it comes to glossy consumer titles concerned with readers' lifestyles, issues with welcoming faces on the cover will sell best. This convention can be seen in all kinds of magazines, but it is most

pronounced in titles aimed at women, where month after month, without exception, every issue confronts the buyer with an image of a beautiful woman. This shot, generally of a model, sometimes of an actress, will show head and shoulders, so that her face fills a large part of the cover, or picture her from the waist up, so that her arms and breasts are visible. The woman will smile, often with open mouth, displaying a row of perfect white teeth. Her hair will be immaculate, her complexion flawless. She will radiate happiness, health and confidence. The images are carefully constructed, with no detail left to chance, but the colour photography – mostly studio-based – is 'neutral' in style, if not in effect. The space around the woman is stacked with cover lines in different sizes, colours (pink, red, orange, yellow) and weights of type, advertising the articles thought most likely to attract the floating buyer: 'Sextasy extra: Double your orgasm satisfaction. The 3 tease-you triggers he must touch tonight' … 'All new love-your-body mind tricks … unleash that inner sinner now!' … 'Revealed: The sneaky chat-up line straight men are using to trick you into bed'. These are all taken from the April 2003 issue of *Cosmopolitan*'s UK edition.

Of course, the problems raised by representing women and their interests and preoccupations in this way are hardly news. Since the early 1970s, feminists have devoted a great deal of analysis to the content of women's magazines.[2] These publications continue to sell in enormous numbers and feminist thinkers struggled to reconcile the pleasure women apparently derived from such images with the role of these images in perpetuating the oppression of women (in the feminist view). However one sees this, one has to acknowledge that the spectacle presented by row upon row of these covers, wherever in the world they are sold – a sight now so banal and universal that it is easily taken for granted – is one of astonishing cross-cultural consistency and conformity.

One need only look at earlier stages in the evolution of women's magazines to appreciate how narrow the visual conventions of the contemporary news-stand have become. A 1940 cover of *Harper's Bazaar*, art directed by Alexey Brodovitch, with a photomontage by Herbert Bayer, already treats female beauty as a fetish, but does so with considerable graphic wit. The woman's face, in delicately overexposed black and white, is repeated eight times; the image's colour comes from her vibrant blue, green, red and yellow lipstick – she has become a kind of proto-Pop-Art multiple. Issues of *Elle* from the 1950s also appealed to women readers by featuring a woman or women on the cover, but a wide range of photographic styles was allowed. While the women conformed to their time's notions of feminine apppearance and behaviour, they were often shown full figure, in different settings, engaging in activities such as driving; they didn't always gaze out at the viewer and nor did they necessarily smile. In the 1960s, the German magazine *Twen*, art directed by Willy Fleckhaus, often showed a single woman's face on the cover, but the models were pictured in many different moods. Despite the emphasis on good looks, which had long since become a convention for such magazines, the women were shown in ways that suggested individuality, independence and an interior life in which sexuality could be acknowledged and enjoyed. Their faces were seen from angles and with expressions – sultry, reflective, withdrawn, even melancholic – that are impossible today. Full-face, open-mouthed smiles were rare. Until the late 1960s, most issues of *Twen* had a single cover line to draw attention to the story felt by the editors to be the most important, and this handful of words became a vital component in brilliantly controlled graphic compositions.[3]

Twen's 1960s British contemporary, *Nova* magazine, went even further.[4] A widely acclaimed news-stand title aimed at the thinking woman, it was prepared to put almost anything on the cover that expressed its journalistic aims. *Nova* ran a picture of pipe-smoking *Playboy* figurehead Hugh Hefner with the legend: 'This man is trying to lure your husband into his burrow.' A cover portrait of a nun holding a Bible bore the quotation: 'There are many roads to perfection … I have tried to explain the way it is for the avowed virgin.' Not until the 1970s did *Nova* regularly resort to showing models on the cover, but even then this iconoclastic publication flew in the face of convention. On a 1971 cover that would be unthinkable now, the model screws up her face and sticks out her tongue at the reader. As the cover line says, 'It's an ugly business being beautiful'.

It is certainly a business. The most successful women's magazines are now global empires. *Cosmopolitan*, already a publishing hit in the US, launched a British edition in 1972. French, Italian, Australian and Mexican editions followed in 1973 and these were later joined by German, Dutch, Spanish, Portuguese, Greek, Turkish, Japanese, Taiwanese, South African, Brazilian, Indian and Russian versions. *Cosmopolitan* has an international vision of what makes an appropriate cover and a *Cosmo* cover girl's picture could be used on editions around the world. These cover designs are utterly formulaic. There is no possibility for editors and art directors to attempt anything different and it is likely that it would not occur to many of those who work on these titles that a cover could look any other way. Research will have shown long ago, to everyone's satisfaction, that this is the type of photograph most readers supposedly want.

If a magazine such as *Nova* attempted to represent the world's complexity and to question the norms of its time, then, by any objective measure, the contemporary women's magazine serves up a breathtakingly truncated version of reality. While the range of articles in some titles is sometimes broader than it appears from the covers, it is still relationships, sex, appearance, clothes and celebrities that dominate. The cover is the single most revealing element because it summarizes the intentions of the whole. It has long been understood by feminist critics that the lifestyles portrayed as desirable in women's magazines do not necessarily reflect the lifestyles and consumption habits of their readers. The magazines serve an aspirational purpose, showing how the reader's life could be improved, as well as offering opportunities for fantasy and escapism. The discrepancy between aspiration and reality is most obvious in the case of the cover image, since few readers will possess this degree of physical beauty and no amount of makeovers, outfit changes and hair colour rethinks will change this fundamental inequality. The reader can hardly be unaware of this fact, but buys the magazine, anyway. Each new issue, no different in essence from the last, drives home the point, even as it pretends to offer solutions to 'problems' that its own content has been instrumental in creating in the reader's mind.

As a man, my view of this is bound to be different from a woman's view. These images are not aimed at me and they cannot provoke the same kind of anxiety that feminists say they provoke in many women, but they are still unavoidable. I buy and read magazines, so I see them all the time. In any case, the corrosive and dispiriting value system they embody with such persistence also pervades other kinds of consumer magazine. Men's titles showing models and film stars on the cover are equally formulaic, the main difference being that they concentrate on the women's skimpily clad bodies. Female flesh is shown from the thighs up and, in this meat market, smiling is beside the point; the model's role is to look like she is offering herself to the buyer. Magazines aimed at teenage and pre-teenage girls apply similarly inflexible cover conventions, encouraging emotionally immature readers to judge themselves, from an early age, in terms of a standard of physical attractiveness that may be unattainable.

For magazine buyers who are attractive, there is little reason why they should give any of this a second thought. It will seem entirely natural that good-looking people – people like themselves – are displayed on magazine covers. The ranks of ravishingly lovely models, beaming dentally flawless smiles from every news-stand, simply confirm what attractive people know in every fibre: that they are the chosen ones, the genetically elect, and that the facially and physically inferior are not so deserving. The politics of attraction are barely considered in our society. The beautiful have nothing to gain from such a discussion and why would the ugly wish to suffer the further humiliation of drawing attention to a genetic misfortune that they have had to learn to live with and would prefer to deny? Only in fiction is the anguish of the unattractive, who know they are despised by the beautiful, sometimes acknowledged. As the controversial French novelist Michel Houellebecq writes in *Whatever*: 'in societies like ours sex truly represents a second system of differentiation, completely independent of money; and as a system of differentiation it functions just as mercilessly.... In a totally liberal sexual system certain people have a varied and exciting erotic life; others are reduced to masturbation and solitude.'[5] Houellebecq's 'extension of the domain of the struggle' (to translate the book's French title) is sexual liberalism: a battle that will produce as many losers as winners. In a short story, the satirist George Saunders imagines these inequalities as the acts of a cruel God, who gives people the need to be liked but denies them the physical and personal attributes that make this possible. 'Having placed his flawed and needy children in a world of exacting specifications, he deducts the difference between what we have and what we need from our hearts and our self-esteem and our mental health.'[6]

The brutal message of these cover images, for many readers, is that in a world of exacting specifications they fall a long way short of perfection. They are simply not good enough. There are hundreds of similar magazines in scores of countries and each one repeats this message on thousands of display racks with 12 new issues every year. There are so many visual stories these publications could choose to tell, but the message they all prioritize is that their readers, who they claim to respect and represent, should aspire to look like, and be like, the model on this month's cover, whether this is feasible or not. Magazines were not always this relentlessly focused in their selection of cover image, as we have seen, but for economic reasons they have evolved to a point where expediency demands that this is the univocal message they express, irrespective of its psychological and social consequences. These front-cover photographs belong to a whole system of similar images delivered by television and advertising and this increases their semblance of normality and their power. One could, with a little effort, see a certain honesty in them. The unequal distribution of attractiveness that they reflect and endorse is one of the realities of being human. If appearances are more important to us than ever, though, it is because we now study them so obsessively and unforgivingly in extreme close-up through the microscope of the media. Behind the brilliant smile, framed by gorgeous glossy lips, the inner reality is increasingly uncertain and dysfunctional. Its full social cost has yet to be calculated.

WHAT DO MEN WANT?

For years Britain's most durable cultural export, held in high regard around the world, was the BBC. Lately, though, as the corporation struggles to redefine its role, some of Britain's most successful media creations have boasted a much less elevated tone. Many American readers and viewers are probably unaware that the men's monthly *Maxim* and the singing talent competition *American Idol* are based on highly popular British formats. *I'm a Celebrity – Get Me Out of Here!* has aired in American and German versions. If you are after lowest common denominator concepts with huge potential to travel, Britain's publishers and TV producers can offer a never-ending supply.

The latest publishing idea, believed to be the first of its kind, is the men's weekly magazine. In January 2004, Britain's already oversupplied news-stands greeted not one but two new titles slugging it out for supremacy. *Zoo*, the first to be announced, is published by Emap, home of FHM, and *Nuts* (no explanation required) is published by IPC, which invented the lad mag with *Loaded* ten years ago.

At first glance the two magazines might seem to be virtually indistinguishable. Both titles have red mastheads with black drop shadows, black bars insisting that they are the best, and covers stuffed with cover lines, photos and a semi-clad woman. But there are subtle distinctions. *Zoo* – '100 pages of girls, football & funny stuff' – is the more gleefully

brainless of the two. 'It's not going to make you think or question things,' confesses editor Paul Merrill, though in the next breath he declares that 'Zoo man' doesn't like to be patronized. He promises a weekly fix of 'all-round stupidity' and delivers the goods in an early issue with an in-depth Christina Aguilera interview ('Sure, I get naked quite a bit'), a charming picture of a Romanian woman with a 12-stone tumour, and page after page of breasts.

By comparison the first issue of Nuts was almost tasteful. There were no pictures of hands sliced up by barbed-wire fences to savour and, apart from some body painting, the women kept their bras on. Nuts makes better use of photographs – one picture story showed an exploding hand grenade in close-up – but both magazines use essentially the same endlessly recycled conventions of mass-market design. Every page is a throbbing patchwork of elements: boxes, captions, coloured panels, numbered paragraphs, dozens of headings. Pictures predominate and even the longest texts are kept short. Nuts has a slightly bigger page and its use of the basic kit of parts is more restrained and carefully handled, giving it a fractionally more upmarket feel.

One easily overlooked aspect of this kind of design is the degree to which quite small amounts of emphasis within the established conventions can be used to position a title for different readerships. These distinctions are particularly apparent in the extensive TV listings that are a key selling point of both titles. Both magazines structure this material in the same way, listing the five main channels on the left-hand page and featuring the day's viewing highlights (from a bloke's point of view) on the right. Zoo's pages are more densely packed, with less white space, a heavier use of coloured bars and tint panels, and less clarity in the division of the listings into horizontal time segments. The coarse-grained pages avoid any suggestion of unmanly prettiness, but they are harder to read. In later issues, Zoo overhauled its TV listings typography, while Nuts responded to its rival's example by boosting the nipple count.

If both magazines aim at 18- to 34-year-olds, then the Zoo reader is probably younger on average, more laddish and less settled, while the Nuts reader is older, has a partner, perhaps a young child or two, a better job and a mortgage. Of course, these are assumptions, but they reflect the calculating way publishers think about their audiences. Editors of lifestyle magazines always claim an intimate knowledge of readers' attitudes and tastes. Commercial publishers, professing to be doing no more than giving these 'niches' what they want, make large suppositions about what people will be interested in, understand or accept.

Photograph:
Fredrika Lökholm

Suggesting that men in this age group have such a narrow range of conventionally masculine concerns and no desire to think is hugely patronizing. Here, design becomes another tool – quite as much as the editorial – by which the audience is classified and targeted. If these products then sell, is it because this really is what men want, or because the evolving conventions of the global marketplace have engineered public taste to respond to this crap?

LIBERATING THE BILLBOARD?

*Trying to Look Good
Limits My Life*, billboard
image (one of five), 2004.
Design: Stefan Sagmeister

We are so accustomed to seeing billboards in the street that they are now taken for granted as an inevitable feature of everyday life. 'No city street would be complete without them,' says John Hegarty of the advertising agency Bartle Bogle Hegarty.[1] According to this view, advertising is central to the purpose and meaning of a city street. If there were empty spaces where the billboards usually go, a street would in some crucial sense not be a proper street at all. Hegarty assumes that our intention in travelling along a street is not merely to get somewhere, but to expose ourselves to a continuous display of messages encouraging us to buy things. Our time, then, as users of this street, is not fully our own. At least some of this time is owed, in the form of our attention, to those who wish to use these billboards to persuade us to part with our money.

In societies that pride themselves on their freedom, this is a remarkable state of affairs. Aside from doubts about the notion that billboards are as natural to a street as trees are to a forest, there are some obvious questions. What gives advertisers the right to impose themselves on us like this as we move around in public? If we are free, then what became of our right not to be treated as a target audience day in, day out everywhere we go? Asking these questions does not necessarily challenge the idea of advertising. Other forms of advertising, at least as it has been practised in the past, are much less intrusive, operating in areas over which the individual can exert a measure of control. You can choose not to buy a magazine full of glossy ads. No one is obliged to watch television and you can always zap between channels. But the billboard presumes to monopolize large areas of shared public space, cluttering the streetscape and blotting the landscape outside towns with its unavoidable appeals.

David Ogilvy, adman and founder of the Ogilvy & Mather agency in New York, openly acknowledged that billboards were indefensible. 'As a private person,' he writes in *Confessions of an Advertising Man*, 'I have a passion for landscape, and I have never seen one which was improved by a billboard. Where every prospect pleases, man is at his vilest when he erects a billboard. When I retire from Madison Avenue, I am going to start a secret society of masked vigilantes who will travel about the world on silent motor bicycles, chopping down posters at the dark of the moon. How many juries will convict us when we are caught in these acts of beneficent citizenship?'[2]

The billboard's immense power to reach the public has inevitably made it a site of struggle. From the 1970s, beneficent citizens who resented the way in which a few outdoor-advertising corporations were allowed to control public spaces began to answer back. They didn't chop the billboards down, but they added messages of their own and changed the ads' meanings, often using nothing more elaborate than a spray can. Later, these Situationist-like acts of *détournement* became more technically, conceptually and graphically sophisticated. The Billboard Liberation Front, formed in San Francisco in the late 1970s, created seamless modifications to roadside billboards using computer-aided design, Photoshop and laser-cut vinyl elements that were pasted into position on the ad. In 1998, this anonymous group of culture jammers targeted Apple computers' 'Think different' advertising campaign, which made use of famous figures. After a simple alteration, the Dalai Lama now advised spectators to 'Think disillusioned', while TV mogul Ted Turner proclaimed 'Think dividends'.

These were acts of semiotic sabotage carried out in secrecy against the wishes of the advertiser, and they survived only as long as the site owner allowed them to remain. But what if it were possible to rent the advertising space and create longer-lasting alternative messages for this most public of platforms? The work of Barbara Kruger is still one of the most striking attempts by an artist to use billboards in this way.[3] In the 1980s and 1990s, with funding from art museums and foundations, Kruger applied a graphic format based on black-and-white photos and a consistent use of the Futura typeface to a series of outdoor projects aimed at car drivers, pedestrians and public-transport users in locations such as New York, Minneapolis, London, Melbourne and Strasbourg. Kruger's slogans had the simplicity, directness and impact of regular advertising copy lines, but their messages were ambiguous and unsettling: 'Surveillance is your busywork'; 'We don't need another hero'; 'L'empathie peut changer le monde' (Empathy could change the world). Showing a perfect understanding of the medium, her work mimics and twists graphic conventions to produce images that are sufficiently 'professional' in appearance to compete on equal terms with conventional advertising and even to overpower it when the two are seen side by side.

There are, however, some problems with this convergence of art and advertising. If artists can become more advertiser-like in their methods, then advertisers, seeking new ways to connect with a jaded public, can become more artistic. In the 1990s, Benetton's controversial campaign, led by creative director and photographer Oliviero Toscani, offered probably the most extreme example to date of the blurring of categories that can occur when a corporation attempts to turn 'artist'. Toscani liked to claim that there was no fundamental difference between what he was doing – showing photographs of a mucus-covered newborn baby or a dying AIDS sufferer next to a Benetton logo on a public billboard – and the commercial underpinnings of publishing and the contemporary art scene.

It was certainly the case that some fine artists were thinking more and more like advertising people. In 2004, in a move that caused jaws to drop in amazement, Kruger collaborated with the Selfridges department store in London on an advertising campaign that looked like a parody of her own artworks. She rendered phrases such as 'You want it. You buy it. You forget it' and her famous 'I shop therefore I am' in her trademark Futura style. Would-be iconoclasts, such as Damien Hirst, made no secret of being excited by advertising's social impact and its power to hold the attention of a broad audience, and they readily embraced the consumerist values it embodied and the mechanisms of promotion it employed. In 1996, in an exhibition at the Larry Gagosian gallery in New York, Hirst displayed a wall-mounted, revolving billboard. One image showed a bulbous cucumber and a jar of Vaseline; another paired a hammer with a peach. Hirst's punch-line – 'The trouble with relationships' – was as short and sharp as any roadside advertising campaign slogan. The tastes of Hirst's patron Charles Saatchi, both Britain's most powerful art collector and an adman, can hardly have failed to influence Hirst and the other artists who depended on Saatchi's support. For publishing projects, such as his 1997 monograph, Hirst chose as his design collaborator Jonathan Barnbrook, who in his early career worked on advertising campaigns with television commercials director Tony Kaye, another exponent of the idea that advertisements should be taken seriously as art and exhibited in museums. In 1999, in collaboration with *Adbusters*, Barnbrook created a Kruger-esque billboard in Las Vegas that carried a slogan by Tibor Kalman: 'Designers ... stay away from corporations that want you to lie for them.'

These interconnections are perhaps sufficient to give a sense of how confused this territory threatens to become. Stefan Sagmeister's billboards for *Art Grandeur Nature* in the Parc de la Courneuve, Paris, in 2004 encapsulate this dilemma vividly. Where Barnbrook's contributions to the outdoor project incline towards an unambiguous statement of his political position – 'Autrefois on marquait les esclaves. Maintenant on est esclaves des marques' (In the past we branded slaves. Now we are slaves to brands) – Sagmeister presents images that leave viewers with a degree of freedom to provide their own interpretations. Where Kruger makes art that dresses in the clothing of design,

Sagmeister produces design that wears the clothing of art. His five billboards, showing a series of outdoor scenes, are linked by words in the images, which form the sentence 'Trying to look good limits my life'. The designer's aim is clearly to encourage us to reconsider our consumerist preoccupation with appearances. Yet there is nothing confrontational or hard to assimilate about these beautifully realized images. They exude a sense of relaxation and contentment. It is all too easy to visualize similarly enigmatic images being used as intriguingly oblique advertisements for an insurance company, an environmentally aware cosmetics retailer, a mobile phone network. Almost anyone could identify with the words 'my life' formed from cactus-like elements stretched on a wire frame in front of an empty football pitch. All the ad would need is a logo in the corner.

The growing art-consciousness of advertising means that any attempt to use the billboard as a medium for serious art simply plays into the ad industry's hands. The more original and effective an idea is as communication, the more likely it is to be appropriated. In the process, distinctions between art and the hard sell become increasingly muddled. For anyone who believes that advertising is the art form of our age, or who thinks there is no vital difference between the two, this will not be a cause for concern. Everyone should be troubled, though, by the omnipresent advertising billboard, especially since the successful precedent that it has set is already sanctioning other even more intrusive forms of advertising. The Spielberg film *Minority Report* offers a future vision of street advertising that uses retinal scanning to produce customized messages for passing consumers. While it is tempting to make use of the billboard as a public delivery system for art projects, and there have been some impressive examples, we know by now that these incursions are unlikely to change anything. It may be that their only effect is to endorse the legitimacy of the medium. The most radical course of action would be to follow adman David Ogilvy's advice, take up arms against the billboard and lobby for its removal from our streets.

LOYALTY BEYOND REASON

'I love Head & Shoulders. I won't buy or use anything else. It's a Lovemark of mine.'[1] By his own admission, the man who wrote this touching tribute to dandruff shampoo has very little hair. He believes, like the Beatles, that 'All You Need Is Love'. He also wants us to know that he has homes in New York, St Tropez and Auckland. His name is Kevin Roberts and he is CEO Worldwide of Saatchi & Saatchi.

It is no secret that branding has become a bore. Once seen as the answer to everything, then attacked by 'no logo' activists as a modern malaise, the notion of the brand is now merely commonplace. If you are in marketing and communications, claiming to offer unique branding solutions is no longer much of a selling point. Saatchi & Saatchi's answer is the 'Lovemark' – nothing less, they claim, than 'the future beyond brands'. Of course, the Lovemark too is actually a brand, but it is a brand that supposedly transcends ordinary brands, a brand able to inspire 'loyalty beyond reason', a brand that creates an intimate emotional connection that its consumers just cannot live without.

Now Roberts has written a book in which he expounds this not very hard to grasp idea at wearying length. *Lovemarks* is by turns wince-makingly sentimental, infuriatingly self-satisfied and intolerably patronizing. Its design suggests that it might be aimed at six-year-olds. Almost every page has key phrases pulled out in large, brightly coloured type. An entire spread is devoted to the word LOVE – yes, it is a big emotion, we get it. Like so many business publications purporting to reveal the way forward, the book is full of statements of the obvious masquerading as special insights.

Three things apparently set a Lovemark apart: mystery, sensuality and intimacy. These are the qualities needed to make a deep emotional relationship and no product or service will attain high levels of respect and love – the hallmark of the Lovemark – without them. But is this an entirely subjective measure or is it intended to have objective value, too? Roberts might regard Head & Shoulders as a Lovemark, but it means nothing to me. On the Lovemarks website, visitors nominate their personal Lovemarks, giving reasons, and then other people vote on them.[2] The implication is that the majority view decides whether something is a Lovemark or not. So all the Lovemark is really doing is identifying the most popular brands in a given sector. If you prefer something else, the concept has nothing useful to say to you.

No matter how much rhetoric Roberts piles on about helping the people and making the world a better place, the fundamental aim remains the same – in his own words, 'huge commercial benefits' and 'premium profits'. The field trips he enthuses about where corporate

Head & Shoulders shampoo, shop display, 2005. Photograph: Sven Herzog researchers go into homes and rummage around in the owners' fridges and laundry baskets are gruesome, and the description of Kodak's marketing to teenagers is equally shameless. 'We need to have an absolutely relentless focus on what's top-of-mind with teens today, because we know their habits change. And we have to remain a beacon to teen girls across the nation, letting them know that it's really okay to be themselves.'[3] Cheers!

It is not enough that business enjoys unwarranted levels of power and influence and bestows vast rewards on the lucky few, while deluging us with idiotic propaganda. It now seeks to present itself as some kind of well-meaning global saviour, even as it tries to annex just about every worthwhile aspect of life – mystery, sensuality, intimacy, love – for commercial purposes. 'At Saatchi & Saatchi,' Roberts reports, 'our pursuit of Love and what it could mean for business has been focused and intense.'[4] If that sentence doesn't make you feel even a little bit queasy, then they have got to you already.

At the Lovemarks site, there is a thing called the Lovemark Profiler. How would Saatchi & Saatchi fare? The first step was to answer four questions with a Yes or No. Was Saatchi & Saatchi the best in its class? Sorry, no. Would I recommend it to a friend? No. Am I confident it wouldn't do anything I wouldn't want to be associated with? Nope. Is it good value for the experience it offers? No, the book isn't. Back came the answer. 'With Lovemarks and respect it's all or nothing.... It doesn't look like Saatchi & Saatchi has the level of respect it needs in order to become a Lovemark.' They said it.

A WORLD WITHOUT ADS

Before you read this, bear with me for a moment and conduct a small thought experiment. Imagine you lived exactly where you live now, in the same circumstances, surrounded by everything you currently take for granted, except for one essential difference. In this alternative world, there are no ads or commercials. Not one. Of course, that would be impossible – we will return to that shortly – but use your considerable powers of visualization and ponder what it would be like. Not a single billboard, or print ad, or street poster, or commercial break interrupting television programmes. Nothing unwanted in the mail. Nothing lurking in the gaps between the steps. Nothing trying to collar your attention when you pay a visit to a public toilet.

Perhaps your mind recoils from such a prospect. Such a world would look totally different from ours. It would seem strangely depleted, denuded even. Advertising is the primary type of imagery in public spaces and all of that would go. Advertising people always insist that all they do is hold a mirror up to society, reflecting who we are, and in this ad-free world we would no longer have this reflection. Would we know who we are without it? Even if you don't like advertising much, you might find yourself resisting this fantasy because you do enjoy some of the ads and even find them useful. If so, in the interest of this little experiment, I ask you to consider whether the chance to be free of the tiresome, distracting babble of messages that mean nothing to you would be compensation enough for the loss of the ads that you like.

Actually, this world, or something close to it, is not hard to enter. Once you leave the developed world, you are in it. Even in central Europe, you can find places that suggest what life without advertising would be like. A few summers ago, I spent a week on a small Croatian island. A few tourists stay there, ferries arrive regularly from the mainland, you can buy a magazine or turn on the TV, but it was pretty much an ad-less week and it felt great, just like it always does. If, in our thought experiment, I had to make a definitive choice – ads or no ads – I would have no hesitation. My interior life would be impoverished in no significant way if I never saw another ad or commercial again.

I stress 'interior' because I accept that, in this economic system, advertising is essential to sell the products that generate the wealth that allows us to buy ever more products. An attack on advertising consequently seems like an attack on our whole way of life. We have lived inside this system for so long that it doesn't occur to most people that it is anything other than the natural way to organize things. Only a minority objects strongly to advertising's intrusions and the people who speak out against advertising today are so few in number that they appear eccentric killjoys who have trouble adapting to the modern world.

Taschen's series of books of all-American ads presented decade by decade demonstrates the intoxicating force of the drug.[1] These seductive volumes cater to what seems to be a deep nostalgia for advertising images of the American dream. Turning their pages, full of sleek, gleaming cars and towering refrigerators overflowing with Technicolor groceries, reveals – more effectively, perhaps, than any academic critique – the power of these images to mould the consciousness of generations of consumers. If these ads didn't and still don't seem like propaganda, which is exactly what they are, it is because people were delighted to be indoctrinated with such palpably wholesome icons of happiness and abundance. For non-Americans, in the 1940s and 1950s, these images promised a fabulous life of then unattainable luxury.

In material terms, many other countries caught up, but America has more advertising on a larger scale than any other economy and the daily experience of commercial persuasion is exceptionally relentless and hard to resist. In a conversation with an American cultural critic whose essays are full of sceptical insights, the subject of advertising came up. He reminisced happily about ads and commercials from his childhood and it was obvious that he loved the stuff. America is a commercial culture, he reminded me, and advertising is its energetic expression.

At a conference in New York, I heard Stuart Ewen, an authority on the development of American advertising, reveal to an audience of designers and design educators, as though it might strike them as news, that a lot of the thinking behind ad campaigns is deeply manipulative. Afterwards, I approached him to express my slight surprise that he felt this needed saying to such a sophisticated group of people. He assured me that it did and I have wondered about this ever since. Was he underestimating his audience or were they as clueless as he implied? *The Hidden Persuaders* appeared as long ago as 1957, after all.[2] As a teenager I understood how advertising worked simply by looking around.

There was a time when some designers used to agonize about where they stood in relation to advertising. Graphic design's origins as a practice may be tied up with advertising – though not exclusively – but there is a world of difference between a poster painted by a commercial artist in the 1920s and the art directed, photographic approaches to advertising that emerged in the 1950s and that have dominated the medium ever since. Photographs showing real, though idealized, people as role models are inherently more coercive and anxiety-forming for the viewer than charmingly stylized representations created by hand. The move to photography (and television) made advertising's purposes plain, as it shed any remaining pretence that it was a form of 'art'. Idealistic young designers starting a career in design in the 1950s were often acutely aware of the dubious nature of so many of advertising's promises. They could see advertising clearly for the propaganda it was. As the British designer Raymond Hawkey explained: 'Both are specifically devised to persuade a sufficiently large number of people that only one given course of action is correct. Both methods make use of half truths and deliberate falsehoods as a means of influencing opinion and appeal to the emotions rather than the intellect. Both rely on being able to tell their audience what it wishes to believe – that the solution to its particular political, professional, domestic or sexual problem is relatively easy, inexpensive and guaranteed. If the audience has no problem it must be given one.'[3]

This was written 50 years ago. We would be more alert to the 'deliberate falsehoods' today (though the phrase is open to interpretation), but apart from that, the situation described by Hawkey is no different now – except that we are more resigned to it and prepared to see it as an inevitable state of affairs. For any designer who finds this intolerable, there is a pressing need to develop ways of working that avoid everything that is false and manipulative about advertising. This issue has received a certain amount of discussion in recent years, but there can never be enough debate because the barrage of propaganda in support of an advertising-led culture continues without cease.

The problem is one of fundamental values. If you accept advertising's picture of reality, its assertions of what matters, its recipes for contentment, its assumed right to treat the populace as a target market, no matter what effect it has on society, then nothing I have said here will make much sense. In London design circles, there has been talk about 'integrated creativity'.[4] This seems to require us to see design and advertising as much the same thing, and to build campaigns where the two forms of communication project a seamlessly consistent image and message. It is another indication of the lack of distance that now exists between the businesses of advertising and design. If the merger succeeds, you might also see it as evidence of design's final capitulation to the priorities of ad-land – a last, desperate bid to survive at any cost.

For anyone who embraces values derived from art, politics, religious conviction, a sense of community or a belief in mutual respect, advertising's world of falsity is a symptom – though not the only one – of everything that has gone wrong in our culture. There is no way that any designer will be allowed to change advertising from the inside, but colluding with it for any length of time is certain to change the designer. This we also know: advertising will continue to inundate us, and in the decades ahead the flood is likely to quicken. We might not be able to banish it from our world, but we can certainly reduce its power to influence our actions by banishing it from our heads.

LOOK AT MY SPEECHTOOL

Poster promoting
***Nathan Barley* sitcom,**
Channel 4, 2005.
Photograph: Rick Poynor

The first time I saw the Wasp T12 Speechtool poster I nearly kept on walking. Could there be a more fatuous idea than calling a mobile phone or cellphone a 'speechtool'? The quote underneath this marketing gem was even more irritating: 'It's well weapon.' The 'well' was bad enough. But now the adjective that usually follows this idiom had been replaced by a noun, to make a phrase that was 'well dickhead'. It was enough to make you want to hurl a copy of *Eats, Shoots & Leaves* at the thing.

Then I noticed the name of the guy brandishing his speechtool at us, Nathan Barley, and the penny dropped. *Nathan Barley* is the title of a new Channel 4 sitcom. Barley, as the poster says, is a 26-year-old 'underground media scoundrel', screenwriter and DJ, as well as a Wasp T12 user. So the poster was a spoof, a teaser for the programme, and a week before the launch it was everywhere. I saw it three times at bus shelters on the way to my local station and again on the platform.

The man behind the poster, comedian and satirist Chris Morris, is one of the most provocative figures working in British TV. His 24-hour-news parody, *The Day Today*, and fake documentary series, *Brass Eye*, savaged media pretensions and pomposities, sometimes – as with a programme about paedophilia – causing a storm of complaints.

Like 'cake', Morris's 'made-up drug' featured in *Brass Eye*, the Wasp T12 is a made-up mobile. And, like his earlier pranks, the poster is so accurately observed, with its plausible yellow slash Wasp logo in the corner, that you could fall for it easily, though the T12's listed functions are ridiculous, given a moment's thought. What would you expect from a phone if not 'full fidelity vox phoning' and what kind of berk would need 'voice authority enhancement' and a 'text insult dictionary'?

But the poster, like the people and products it lampoons, is about attitude and Nathan Barley has plenty of that. Wasp's slogan is 'Hoot your trap off' and Nathan looks like someone who would jump at a text insult facility, while the T12, with its scuffed, hazard-tape patina and shark-like outline, does resemble some kind of weapon. At the website given on the poster the joke is extended to new levels of absurdity.[1] The narrow display is 'compressed wide screen', the keypad features every known integer – well, it would – and a facility called 'intelligent thermotones' allows you to rate caller IDs according to coolness. The T12's design is a 'subversively cool-shape style-shape'.

The poster is a particularly seamless piece of culture jamming. I saw it next to an Orange mobile network ad, with the slogan 'Send 2 texts 4 the price of 1', and it looked like the real thing. Its purpose may be to promote the programme, but it reads primarily as a sardonic swipe at manipulative lifestyle branding aimed at young people, and this anti-consumerist message has the benefit, for once, of hundreds of locations. The idea is so unfamiliar, though, that many viewers may have overlooked it. We just don't expect this kind of dissent at the bus stop and it would be easy, if you dislike crass ads, to blank it out, as I nearly did myself. It is doubtful, too, whether anyone who felt inspired to try to buy a T12 would be shaken out of their infatuation with cool technology by discovering it was a hoax, but that is their problem.

As an ad for the programme, the poster's effectiveness may have been limited. The sitcom is not mentioned by name and there are no transmission details. The reference to Channel 4 is so subtle that it took me a while to realize it contained one at all. The '4' on the keypad, a tiny area of the poster surface, represents the Channel 4 logo.

That just adds to the poster's interest as a new kind of subvertising. One of the strengths of *Brass Eye* was its astute parody of the self-important and melodramatic TV graphics used for sensationalistic news programmes and documentaries. Morris's scorn verges on nihilism and the rightness of these supporting details helps to give his satires their Swiftian bite. When it came to *Nathan Barley*, questions arose about whether its mocking picture of the new media scene in Shoreditch, London, was five years out of date. That was for the sitcom's viewers to decide. But the poster hits the right keys and does it within a framework usually unavailable to this kind of satirical message.

THE CITIZEN DESIGNER

Corporate American Flag,
protest graphic for
***Adbusters*, 2003.**
Design: Shi-Zhe Yung

By the end of the 1990s, anyone who felt that corporate power was getting out of hand had good reason to be hopeful. After a long period of complacency, public discussion was starting to happen in the US and other liberal democracies, spurred by expressions of disaffection seen at a series of protests, beginning with the World Trade Organization negotiations in Seattle in 1999, and fuelled by the appearance of books such as Naomi Klein's *No Logo* and Thomas Frank's *One Market Under God*. Some designers, too, were showing signs of unrest. By the late 1990s, *Adbusters* had become a must-read publication for many, and the magazine's launch of the *First Things First 2000* manifesto gave additional focus to this renewed questioning of design's position in the scheme of things.

The plans made by the American Institute of Graphic Arts (AIGA) for its national design conference, 'Voice', in late September 2001 seemed set to give further impetus to design's questioning mood. In retrospect, the decision to cancel the event, following 11 September, was unquestionably correct, but it is emblematic of the way that, since that terrible moment, the discussion of formerly pressing issues such as globalization has been pushed aside. Considered as news events, concerns about sweatshop exploitation and advertising in schools paled in comparison with thousands of dead, anthrax scares, the defence of the free world and the bombing of Afghanistan. Anyone speaking out against corporate domination ran the risk of being branded a terrorist sympathizer, but in the aftermath of 9/11, as we came to terms with the shock and remembered the victims, few people were listening anyway. Enron was portrayed as the wrongdoing of a few bad apples rather than as a disturbing sign of precisely the kind of systemic corruption and failure that the anti-globalization protesters had been talking about. Before long the issue that overrode all others was Iraq.

It was hardly surprising that, for well-meaning attendees and participants at the rescheduled 'Voice 2' in March 2002, 9/11 continued to loom large. For some designers, especially for those who live and work in New York, the destruction provoked a profound need to find a way to use their design skills to contribute. 'Many designers in and out of New York, feeling they had a public responsibility, produced images and words to help us deal with this unprecedented event,' Milton Glaser told the conference.[1]

These are sentiments with which anyone can identify, but in terms of the broader issues – the issues that preoccupied many concerned people before 9/11 – they don't take us very far. While the hurt must be addressed, addressing it will not in itself bring about deeper change. More worryingly, the emotional bond that comes from shared distress and fear is easily manipulated by political forces with a vested interest in avoiding more searching and potentially troublesome forms of introspection and inquiry. In this climate, even the mildest forms of self-reproach from America's internal critics generated accusations of betrayal and appeasement from those who would like us to believe that the only available course is to unite in the face of a common enemy. Only now is a wider range of responses beginning to be heard.

It has to be said that designers were not, even before 9/11, conspicuous supporters of the anti-capitalist movement. I confess that I hesitated as I wrote 'anti-capitalist' out of concern that using such a phrase – shorthand for a complicated mixture of causes and interests – might seem too politicized, too leftist, too doctrinaire, too off-putting. The problem that dogs all analysis of these issues as they relate to design is that, at root, these are political questions. Any discussion that fails to acknowledge this will never move very far beyond vague, platitudinous statements of a desire to 'improve things'.

One of design's great visionaries, Buckminster Fuller, believed that these issues were so important that they bypassed the trivialities of mere politics. Fuller was right about many things, but on this point he was wrong. There may be more than enough resources in the world to go around, as he often pointed out, but human beings do not spontaneously opt for what he saw as the fair and rational course of action and share them out. Politics is the only mechanism by which a more equitable arrangement might be achieved. Yet to state the essentially political nature of the challenge not only risks alienating designers who do not feel themselves to be political creatures, or who see design as somehow existing apart from politics, but actively antagonizes those who do not share these political views. Perhaps at this point we should simply accept this, because the key issue, put starkly, concerns what we as a society most value and how we wish to live. If you do not acknowledge the reality of the struggle for political power, which will proceed regardless, you simply play into the hands of those who have no compunction in exploiting your lack of 'voice'.

So design badly needs people ready to stand up and speak out. We have a few, but they tend to be lone figures and mavericks, image-makers such as Shawn Wolfe in the US or Jonathan Barnbrook in the UK. While some argue with alarming vehemence that such work achieves nothing apart from letting off steam and publicizing the designer, I believe that it has considerable value. The consumerist status quo pumps out a vast, overwhelming, massively resourced slurry of consciousness-shaping propaganda. What on earth is wrong in producing and taking support from some alternative points of view?

On its own, though, this will never be enough. The fundamental question for design, now and for ever, is how it should relate to the public, and this was a point made persuasively at 'Voice 2' by Samina Quraeshi, Professor in Family and Community at the University of Miami. Design has a central role, she noted, in 'breaking down the physical and psychological barriers to full participation in society' and giving citizens 'the means to express their needs and solve their problems'.[2] This point was taken up in one of the short texts written in response to the conference. It is the designer's responsibility, says Sheri Koetting of New York, to engage society: 'Society depends on citizen participation, and information design holds the key.'[3] At the end of her talk, Quraeshi challenged the audience 'to become architects of change'. The first step for the citizen-designer, she said, is to develop an understanding of the changes under way in the world and of the many cultural values and traditions that give worth to human life. The next step lies in individual action at community level. 'Begin in the home, move to the street, reach out to the neighbourhood, restore the community, re-imagine the world ...' Quraeshi concluded. 'The architecture of change depends upon an enlightened design community.'[4]

This is easy to say and many of us, seeing ourselves as already enlightened, would probably endorse it as a statement of principle. But to redefine design in terms of Quraeshi's model would require nothing less than a complete reversal of the way in which we think about and employ design most of the time. Once again, there is no way around it: this is a political question. Even to begin to understand changes in the world, you need a conceptual framework in which to view them; merely witnessing or experiencing these changes does not mean you understand them, even if you are able to reflect them in your work. Any interpretation of these changes that you use as the basis for your own actions will be informed by an underlying ideology of some kind whether you recognize it or not.

Once you move out into the street, you are already entering a contested terrain, since the street, as hardly needs restating here, is increasingly treated not as a civic space in which an active community defines its own needs and priorities and expresses itself in its own way, but as a commercial space whose purpose is to sell things to herds of essentially passive consumers. Rampant commercial forces have played a huge part in damaging neighbourhoods (as in the Wal-Mart effect on town centres) and demoralizing our sense of what full engagement in the public realm might mean. Any attempt to restore a community and give it back a sense of itself will need to challenge these colonizing forces with a vigorous alternative vision of urban organization endorsed by political backing at both local and national levels. If the task of re-imagining just one blighted, dysfunctional city seems vast, then how much more imponderable Quraeshi's exhortation to 're-imagine the world'?

Small wonder that so many designers prefer to find solace in the private world of their screens: a realm they can fully control. Nevertheless, daunting as the task of citizen-designer might sound, Quraeshi offers some challenging speculations about design's potential role. Designers, she argues, have a unique skill-set, vital to the contemporary world, and this is their capacity for interdisciplinary thinking, which allows them 'to see the multifaceted nature inherent in any problem'. New opportunities to apply a designerly way of problem-solving are emerging in private, public and non-profit sectors. Bruce Mau says similar things about his Institute Without Boundaries educational venture. These are large, rather self-aggrandizing claims, but without such a level of self-belief (backed up by real ability) there is no way in which designers will ever exert fundamental influence. Essential to this, as Quraeshi notes, is a willingness to mix with civic leaders, appointed officials and volunteers, who frequently come from the business community served by design.

On this point, one of the responses prompted by 'Voice 2' was particularly instructive. Bennett Peji, a former president of the AIGA's San Diego chapter, reported how, in less than a decade, the chapter has evolved from a professional organization to a service organization 'whose mission is to utilize design for the public good'. Peji puts 20 hours a week into running his business and 20 hours into voluntary work, serving on the board of five non-profit organizations. 'The key to truly affecting any group's design perspective,' he says, 'is to effect change by serving on the board, not just being a pro bono vendor.'[5] He cites the example of the San Diego Dance Institute, now renamed CityMoves with his prompting, and describes how this kind of organization can be awakened to the power of design as a tool for defining and expressing its activities and goals. In the 1990s, the San Diego chapter rallied a complacent design community, tripled its membership and gave its support to city art programmes at the service of disadvantaged neighbourhoods. From this position of strength, the chapter continues to forge alliances with other creative professionals in the area. The aim, says Peji, is to build a creative community with political influence in

San Diego. 'Design is not the end goal,' he notes. 'Design is simply a tool to help us connect to our communities and make a difference.'[6]

That simple statement encapsulates a profound and, perhaps for many, rather alarming challenge to design. If we are honest, so much of the design we produce and acclaim and obsess over seems to exist primarily for itself. The client often comes a not-so-close second and the public, let alone the public good, doesn't really figure in the reckoning at all. In his conference talk, Milton Glaser drew attention to the AIGA's new code of ethics, which offers information about appropriate behaviour towards clients and other designers, 'but not a word about a designer's relationship to the public'.[7]

For anyone who believes that this relationship is the heart of the issue, it should be a matter of urgency now to act. Designers are much too insular. If you really wish to be an architect of change, you cannot go it alone. Those who support the idea of reform should do more to connect with like-minded colleagues, both inside and outside design. There is strength in numbers and, more than anything, we need coalitions, pressure groups, proposals and plans. We should think much more strategically about how to press design's case where it counts most – in the places where power resides. We must ensure that design, as an interdisciplinary way of thinking, becomes an integral and equal component of significant public initiatives. There is no other way.

RAMSHACKLE UTOPIAS

From my window, in the room where this is being written, I can see the allotments. When I arrived here, several years ago, I didn't give them much thought. Allotments seemed like relics of some earlier austerity Britain, when the population was enjoined to plant potatoes and cabbages and 'Dig for Victory'. They were places where old boys with nothing better to do pottered about with forks and compost and flasks of tea. Today, it is raining and there is nobody there. Occasionally, on the far side, a train will pass at eye level along a bank overgrown with buddleia and weeds, where the foxes live. The birds like the allotment, too. On a dry day they glide and swoop above the land, but now the only movement comes from the gentle rhythm of rain on leaves and the breeze that ruffles the tinfoil bird-scarers on strings. It didn't take me long to realize that unless I fitted a blind to block out this leafy rectangle, I could lose hours each day gazing out of the window at the comings and goings below.

In the last few years, the public image of allotments has changed. They are becoming fashionable among the unlikeliest groups of people. In an article in the *Guardian*, assorted academics explained how, to take a break from cogitation, they liked nothing better than to cultivate their own asparagus, broccoli, brassica and carrots.[1] In 1998, in its report *The Future of Allotments*, the Environment, Transport and Regional Affairs

Committee concluded that there was an 'emerging renaissance' in demand.[2] Contrary to the traditional image of the plot-holder as a retired man, only 35 per cent are 65 or over; 30 per cent are 50–64 and 35 per cent are under 50. Between 1969 and 1993, the proportion of women plot-holders increased from 3 to 16 per cent, but the actual figure for women allotment gardeners is likely to be considerably higher, since women often tend plots registered in a male partner's name. However, while demand apparently increases, provision continues to fall. In 1943, at the height of the war effort, there were 1,400,000 allotments. By 1970, this had dropped to around 500,000. Since then a further 250,000, most of them council-owned, have been lost.

The demand for land puts these sites under enormous pressure. The UK needs to build around 4.5 million homes by 2015. Allotment sites that were once on the urban periphery are now within the limits of development, and developers eye the land hungrily. To them, it must look like potential profit frittered away. Gardeners lucky enough to occupy a plot receive an exceptional benefit for a negligible investment. In my borough, a small plot of 5 rods (approximately 125 square metres) costs the plot-holder just £33 per year and a 10-rod plot (250 square metres) costs only £66.

People are turning to allotments again in response to concerns about food safety, the high cost of organic produce sold by supermarkets, and the continuing national passion for gardening. But one of the more noteworthy aspects of allotments is the model of spatial – and therefore of social – organization that they represent. Strangers occupy defined but physically borderless territories within a shared tract of land. What is planted and the way that a plot is laid out and subdivided is at the discretion of the individual (subject only to a few minor local authority restrictions). It might be argued that this is no different, in essence, from what happens on a larger scale in a street full of gardens, but gardens are privately owned spaces held apart by fences, walls and planting. An allotment site, by contrast, is a collective space, open and permeable. Everyone is free to wander along the narrow pathways between plots and, just as crucially, the sight lines across the allotments as a whole are continuous – you cannot, politely, stare into people's back gardens. One of the great pleasures of traversing a site is the huge variety of plot layouts and features within the framework of the underlying grid, and appreciating that these are expressions not of large-scale impersonal forces, but of individual preference, taste and whim.

There is something in the open culture of allotments that encourages the way of thinking that Claude Lévi-Strauss called 'bricolage'. In

Allotment, 2000.
Photograph: Rick Poynor

folk cultures, the bricoleur 'makes do' when constructing something and extemporizes a solution from whatever materials come to hand. In modern technological cultures, however, tasks are subordinated to the availability of raw materials and tools are procured and conceived for the purposes of the project.[3] The goal-directed products of contemporary engineering – garden tools, lawnmowers, strimmers – can naturally be found on allotments, but they coexist with assemblages patched up and lashed together from humble, even degraded materials that could not be further removed from the decorous outdoor ornaments sold in a garden centre: a low-level barrier, not quite a fence, constructed from a thin concrete slab, a corrugated panel and a chunk of wire mesh; a rickety cage, to keep the birds away, cobbled together from bamboo poles, plastic netting, string and wooden clothes pegs; a miniature lean-to 'greenhouse' fashioned from cast-off window frames, shedding scaly flakes of paint; a do-it-yourself support structure for a raspberry bush that bristles with different weights of iron pole, like a rusting armoury of pikes and muskets. The detritus of everyday consumer culture collides with the allotment economy of recycling and bricolage to form surreal graphic totems. Empty Lenor fabric-softener bottles and Pringles crisps tubes jiggle on the end of bamboo canes, and unwanted CD-ROMs for a ten-hour Internet trial, iMac essentials and First Direct banking flutter in the wind.

In their gentle way, allotments may be one of our most subversive social spaces. The beleaguered allotment site is a small-scale, ramshackle utopia created by citizen-gardeners from all walks of life. Its values – self-sufficiency, mutual aid, inner quiet and deep communion, expressed through the body's exertion, with natural cycles of growth – are fundamentally at odds with the manufactured reality, instant consumer gratifications and atomization of society outside the gate. Allotments are always vulnerable to break-ins and vandalism, but levels of trust among gardeners are high. Forks, hoes and trowels are left where they were last used, waiting for the plot-holder's return. Allotments are one of the few public spaces where, working alongside others in shared voluntary endeavour, it is possible to snatch a few hours away from the buzzing distractions and sensorial overload of contemporary life. Nothing would look more incongruous or misconceived on an allotment than an advertising billboard. The more insistent and vacuous the media hubbub becomes, the more the allotment's unmediated simplicities are perceived as a refuge and luxury. In an era when 'intelligent' vehicles, buildings and clothing are presented as the logical next step for tool-using man, a boon to be welcomed by all, it is

Allotment, 2000.
Photograph: Rick Poynor

remarkable that such a degree of fulfilment is still to be had from fixing a piece of netting to a pole with a handful of pegs and watching your tomatoes ripen in the sun. 'It's the organicity of it, I suppose – the earthy wholesomeness – contrasted with the near sterility of professional activity,' notes Dr Chris Pinney, anthropologist and allotment-holder. 'It's the desire to escape the alienation of wage labour to temporarily inhabit this idyllic world where you control the lifecycle. It's wonderfully satisfying.'[4]

As *The Future of Allotments* recognized, for many allotment-holders their plot forms a fundamental part of their lives. Long-term plot-holders develop especially deep attachments to their land. One local man has had his double-allotment for 36 years. I see him there almost every day. His father had it before him. The inner recesses of his intricately landscaped plot are a sanctuary, with a neatly trimmed strip of lawn, two apple trees and an old, lopsided wooden bench. The Select Committee's report found that allotment gardening had considerable therapeutic value and made a significant contribution to both physical and mental good health. 'I have lived in flats all my life and currently live on a busy council estate,' explained one plot-holder. 'I have no hope of ever being able to afford a garden, since my work is rather low status and underpaid … My allotment has enabled me to find a side of myself I did not know existed and it also helps me cope with an extremely stressful job in a stressful city.'[5]

The report concluded that the benefits allotment sites provide to both allotment holders and the public mean that they have a 'critical role in modern, urban life'. It argued that there is an urgent need to protect existing sites and urged government to clarify the role it sees for allotments in the future. Its recommendations covered changes in legislation, policy and practice and it suggested that the force of these measures would be lost if a piecemeal approach was adopted to their implementation. The government's fence-sitting response was to endorse many of these recommendations on paper, while declining to support them in practice with new legislation.[6]

Looking out of my window, I am acutely aware of the temporality of this privileged patch of land. It has been here for decades, it is highly cultivated, yet it still feels provisional – under threat. To some ways of thinking, pockets of space like this don't make planning sense in built-up areas. Allotments don't pay their way. The site is the perfect size for a cul-de-sac of smart new houses. The industrial estate that borders one side would love to get its hands on it, so far without success. One day some canny developer will succeed and another green space will be expunged from London's map. The problem, as always, is that the qualities and ideas many of us most value are often the hardest to explain or justify in cost-accounting terms. What makes an area pleasant to live in for many people are the open spaces between the buildings, as much as the buildings themselves, and it is slowly becoming more widely understood that the value of housing (in both senses) is linked to the ratio of built environment to green space. I don't have an allotment, but I know that I have gained immeasurably by overlooking this site. Allotment gardening is more than just a 'worthwhile leisure activity', as the government put it, on a par with camping or golf. Allotments are unique collective works, evolving organic tapestries to which many hands contribute. They offer a model of sustainable living, with much larger implications, at a time when this should be a national priority in a country with vision. Allotment gardeners: the new utopians? It has finally stopped raining and people are returning to their plots.

MR HANCOCK'S NEW WAVE ART CLASS

Beauty Stab by ABC, album cover, Neutron, 1983. Painting and design: Keith Breeden

Over the years, Malcolm Garrett and Peter Saville have often mentioned in interviews that they studied together at Manchester Polytechnic in the 1970s. Less well known, though it sometimes comes up in passing, is that they also attended the same school, St Ambrose College, an independent Catholic grammar in Hale Barns, Cheshire. Barely remarked at all is that Keith Breeden, a third, not so renowned contributor to Britain's graphic 'new wave', was a member of the same A level art class. At school, as both Saville and Garrett affirm, Breeden was a significant influence on them. The only known photograph of the three fledgling designers in the school art room is printed tantalizingly small in Saville's monograph, *Designed by Peter Saville*.

It is odd that more has not been made of this surprising confluence of talent. In a class of just six teenagers taking art, half of the group went on to devote their efforts to album cover design and two became leading figures with national and international reputations. Where many once-celebrated new wave design teams of the early 1980s – Rocking Russian, Shoot That Tiger, Town and Country Planning – are all but forgotten now, Saville and Garrett have stayed the course. The national press coverage generated by the Saville monograph and the Design Museum's retrospective – even the ultra-highbrow *London Review of Books* was moved to break its usual silence on design – confirmed just how deeply his work affected those who consumed it at the time.

It is still too early, though, to determine with any precision how significant the impact of Garrett and Saville was for British design. Saville's book and exhibition excited impressionistic claims by journalists that his designs had ignited a taste revolution in the high streets of Britain and, unsurprisingly, Saville was ready to agree. It would take a detailed examination of many kinds of evidence to ascertain whether this claim stands up, and this is a task for future design historians. What can be said with more certainty is that many designers do acknowledge that they have been influenced by Saville – as much perhaps by his example as by his work.

With the passage of time, the details of Garrett's role in the British new wave have become a little blurred. He used the visibility it gave him to evolve in other directions. He was an early advocate in Britain of the use of computers in graphic design and, in 1994, he co-founded AMX to concentrate on design for new media. Garrett built the sort of bridges with the design industry that Saville has never seemed to value or want. He involved himself in design education and became a visiting professor at the Royal College of Art. In 2000, he received the ultimate sign of establishment recognition when he was made a Royal Designer for Industry, for his achievements in new media, alongside such long-serving stalwarts as Alan Fletcher, Derek Birdsall and Mike Dempsey.

Saville, for his part, is quite certain about what he owes to Garrett, often mentioning him in interviews about his early days. 'I was definitely influenced by Malcolm,' he insists. 'Malcolm was my cultish muse and connection [with the esoteric] and he was so through college. Malcolm fed me. I was able to learn through his inquisitiveness.' Their close friendship has clearly had a lasting impact on both.

A year older than Garrett and Breeden, Saville moved into the second year at St Ambrose College in 1967, when they were starting first year, at the age of 11. St Ambrose was run by the Irish Christian Brothers and, as Saville recalls, in the early 1960s, a new headmaster acquired the funds to extend it. Catholic schools draw in pupils from a large catchment area and the head realized that he would need more local boys to gain local support for the school. He canvassed the area for pupils of any faith, which is how Saville – non-practising Church of England – came to start at the St Ambrose prep school at the age of seven, rather than following his older brothers to boarding school.

While Saville lived locally, in Hale, Garrett and Breeden, both Catholics, made the 24-kilometre (15-mile) trip each day by train from Northwich. There were other differences, too. Saville came from a well-off middle-class family. 'I grew up with a lot of *objets d'art* around me. There were some paintings in the house. There was a lot of antique furniture.' Garrett lived in a council house and Breeden lived a bike ride away on a Wimpey housing estate. It was several years before Saville and Garrett became friendly and Saville and Breeden were never close. 'He was an odd bod, to me,' says Breeden. 'He was a bit remote and distant.' One point of contact, by the third or fourth form, was slot cars. Saville built and painted cars with designs inspired by pictures in custom-car magazines and travelled around the country to race them. Garrett also built models, and he and Breeden would watch motor races at the Oulton Park track.

Rock music was an obsession, as it was for many teenagers in the early 1970s, to a degree that is hard to imagine now there are so many other competing forms of entertainment. Garrett and Breeden both describe playing truant so they could go to the back door of the Manchester Free Trade Hall and help the roadies carry in equipment for concerts by Free, Pink Floyd, Hawkwind and many other bands. 'For me,' says Garrett, 'Barney Bubbles [Hawkwind's designer] and the whole Hawkwind thing satisfied so many questions: interest in music and music as a lifestyle that embraced an understanding and control of your whole visual persona.' They wore the rebel uniform of the time: school-rule-flouting, shoulder-length hair and flares. 'Malcolm was a show-off, really. Everybody had Afghan coats, but he had to have the king of Afghan coats,' remembers Breeden. 'I think Malcolm had more of a bent towards being controversial,' says Saville. 'Definitely a bit more angst than I had. My life was more comfortable and spoilt than Malcolm's.' Saville, too, was absorbed by rock, though he didn't buy an album of his own until Garrett – a 'Krautrock' fanatic – introduced him to Kraftwerk's *Autobahn* in 1974.

All three were committed to art. 'I always knew from before going to St Ambrose that my career was going to be in art somehow,' says Garrett. 'I assumed it was going to be architecture.' Garrett, like Saville a year ahead of him, was an academically promising 'A stream' pupil, and both took their English and maths O levels a year early. At A level, Garrett studied art, physics and maths – subjects suitable for architecture – while Saville took art and, with dwindling levels of application, geography and English. Their art teacher, P.D. Hancock (usually known by his middle name, David), had arrived at St Ambrose in 1968, at the age of 22, after studying graphic design at Newport College of Art and secondary school teaching at Manchester University. He taught at the school for 29 years, before retiring in 1997.

Today, Saville and Garrett seem to have forgotten Hancock's design background, or perhaps they were never fully aware of it, but it explains both the type of projects he gave them and his eventual suggestion, which Saville recalls, that they should study graphics. 'As I did graphic design,' says Hancock, 'I geared the whole department towards that whereas someone who'd done sculpture would have ordered kilns and done more 3D work.' Saville realized just how open Hancock's approach had been when he met other students during his foundation year and found they had never been allowed to do a piece of abstract work. 'He was definitely pretty hip,' says Saville, 'so this was quite exciting, and he brought a lot of fresh and very liberal ideas to the art course.' With Hancock, the students produced collages, colour-field paintings and other kinds of abstraction, as well as design projects incorporating hand-lettering and typography. Saville, inspired by airbrush illustrations he had seen in magazines, wanted to use an airbrush and Hancock bought one for the school. The A level syllabus was divided into still life, pictorial composition and history of architecture (rather than history of art), which introduced them to modernism and the Bauhaus.

It wasn't until the sixth form that Saville and Garrett began to spend a lot of time with each other. The upper and lower sixth worked together. In addition to lessons, they would put in extra time doing art in free periods and after school. Saville broke his leg in a motorcycle accident and ended up repeating a year of the sixth form, so he took his A levels in 1974 at the same time as Garrett. Saville received an E pass, Garrett an A. Breeden, the most disaffected and rebellious of the three – Garrett remembers him as a 'driven loner' – left school early without taking the exams.

Pop Art was the single biggest influence on their visual aspirations, although it was an awareness filtered through other sources. For Garrett and Breeden, it was embodied above all in late-1960s psychedelia and rock record sleeve design. Both Garrett and Saville cite *The Velvet Undergound & Nico* (1967), with its vibrant stylized banana, signed by Andy Warhol, as a key image. Here was a band produced and presented by a visual artist as part of his own concept and show, *The Exploding Plastic Inevitable*. Saville recalls the importance of colour supplements as a source of information about Pop Art painters. Hancock didn't like Pop Art much, so this was not something he encouraged, though he filled an art-room cupboard with art books, which he bought for the department, and recalls showing them Warhol's soup tins and Monroe screen prints, as well as other kinds of art. Garrett cites Lucy R. Lippard's *Pop Art* (1967), borrowed from a friend at another school, as the first book he read about Pop. It contained a reproduction of *Custom Painting No. 3* (1965) by the British Pop painter Peter Phillips, and Phillips became the most significant influence on both Garrett and Saville, who later wrote his degree thesis about the artist. 'We loved his hard edge,' says Garrett. Phillips's clinically graphic details of helmets, dashboards and car bodies made perfect sense to these racing-car enthusiasts (Garrett later collected 1960s American cars). They were envious of Breeden's ability to produce his own effortlessly accomplished versions of Phillips – 'Whatever Keith was drawing or painting was topic of the week,' says Saville – though a more inspirational figure for Breeden was American Pop artist James Rosenquist, painter of the 26-metre (86-foot) mural *F-111* (1965).

Neither Garrett nor Saville pursued their interest in Pop Art in an academic way, and they didn't see any originals until after they had left school. For Garrett, fine art was too closely identified with the Establishment and he had little desire to venture into galleries. In 1974, he began to study typography and graphic communication at Reading

University, while Saville stayed in Manchester to do his foundation year at Manchester Polytechnic before starting graphic design. For the first time, during that academic year, they separately visited the Whitworth Art Gallery in Manchester, where they discovered that ten Marilyn screen prints by Warhol had been near at hand all along. 'I would have been less shocked if a UFO had landed,' says Saville. 'I was just absolutely stunned that they were there.' Garrett, too, was overwhelmed. 'That was my first real experience of the power of fine art in a gallery, but I was still anti-art and I was sort of anti-academia as well.' In 1976, this time together, they visited an exhibition of prints by Peter Phillips at the Tate Gallery, London. (In 1982, art critic Marco Livingstone, in a nicely intuitive piece of commissioning, asked Garrett to design the catalogue for a Peter Phillips travelling exhibition, 'retroVision'.)

As Garrett and Saville now acknowledge, their reading of Pop was based on a fundamental misunderstanding. 'We've talked about this, actually,' says Saville. 'We thought that Pop was the fine-art endorsement of the aesthetic that appealed to us – as art. So Pop was saying that a custom car was art. Pop was saying that the iconography of consumerism that we liked so much was art. So a painting of an ice-cream cone is art now; it was an ad or a poster and now it's art.' They came to realize that Pop, some of which set out to critique the graphic language of commercial culture, wasn't the uncomplicated celebration they took it to be. Their early interpretation was, after all, based only on reproductions and a superficial sense of what these artists were about. 'The reproduction of those paintings made them sharper and flatter coloured and more hard edged and more graphic than they were,' notes Garrett. Pop's presumed endorsement of 'graphics' simply confirmed they were on the right path.

Breeden, meanwhile, was trying to escape from design. After a difficult foundation year at Northwich Art School – 'I was a total waster,' he admits. 'I didn't get on.' – he applied, in 1974, to study fine art at Bath Academy of Art, Corsham. The work he presented was in a hyperrealist, Pop Art idiom and he was told that he could only be admitted to study graphic design. Breeden accepted the offer, but found the course 'dull and pointless' and left during the first year. He returned a year later, only to quit again. He drifted around, supporting himself with gardening, grave digging, and painting pictures of pubs and people's houses whenever anyone asked. It is clear that he had a talent for painting, but he lacked direction and had no idea how to apply it.

At Reading, despite his nail varnish and outré wardrobe – witnesses still recall his silver boots – Garrett's development was taking a more rigorous course. He studied art history and psychology, learnt how to use a library and started to read more seriously. He gained a practical grounding in typography, type design, bookbinding and use of the darkroom, and sharpened his skills of observation and analysis using drawing. History of art bored him in the main, except for Pop, Dada and Surrealism. A friend studying French literature introduced him to Maurice Nadeau's classic *The History of Surrealism* and he saw an exhibition of original Dadaist pieces around this time. Later, he produced a series of Dadaist/Surrealist manifestos of his own. For one project, he wanted to redesign the inner sleeve typography of Bowie's *Ziggy Stardust*, which he considered poorly done, but his tutor dissuaded him. 'Michael Twyman [his professor] hated record-sleeve design,' Garrett says. 'It wasn't real design.' He ended up failing art history. 'I wrote "Dada" on my exam paper and I walked out after half an hour.' He passed second time around, but he wasn't inspired by the work he could see fourth-year students doing and Saville seemed to have more freedom to pursue their shared pop culture obsessions at Manchester Polytechnic.

In October 1975, Garrett joined Saville for the first year of the graphic design course. At school, they had spent many hours talking about music, design, fashion and art, and the dialogue continued through their three years at the poly. 'We'd sit outside my flat for an hour and a half or more in his car,' says Garrett. 'Those conversations just went on and on.' As Saville describes it, they shared a vision of what might be possible in design. 'Malcolm and I did have a master plan,' he says. 'It was a very innocent, idealistic and naive master plan, probably the same master plan that many young, hopeful designers have. There are periods when you love everything around you and want to be part of it, and there are periods when you don't love what's around you and you want to change it. We were lucky that the mid-1970s punk period was one of those moments and we wanted to change it.'

Even at school, Garrett explains, Saville displayed 'this sense of where things were positioned, the sense that the time is right for something; this is how things should fit into the flow of things.' Yet, despite Saville's suggestion of a joint mission, Garrett has never possessed Saville's single-minded focus and certainty. He has the more inclusive mentality of a curator or collector, but he has also retained the enthusiasm of the true fan. His attention is pulled in so many directions by competing alternatives that he can find it hard to make a choice. 'I knew

Mr Hancock's new wave art class

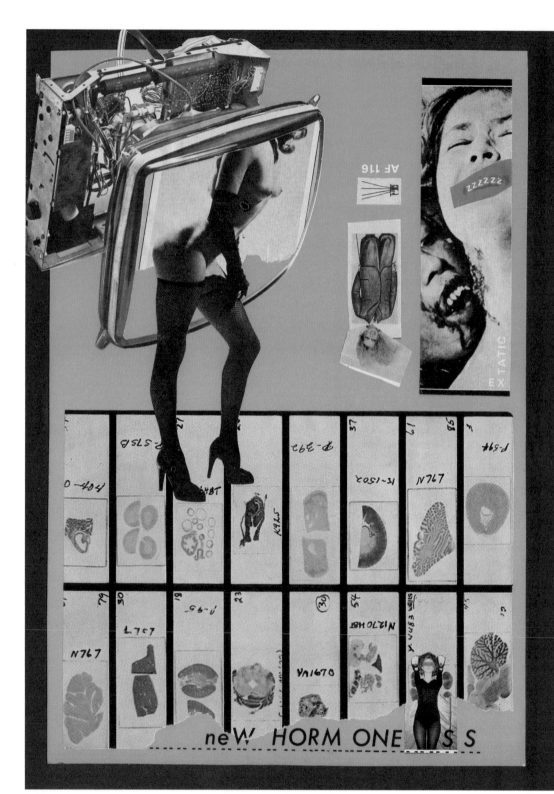

that my interests were many and varied,' says Garrett, 'and I was trying to find a vehicle that was making a statement, but I was also aware that this statement was a little bit scattergun, which is why I love the whole Dada thing.' Saville recalls that when Garrett arrived back in Manchester, he was armed with avant-garde source material – a 'secret weapon' – that was unfamiliar to other students. 'Malcolm had already looked at Dadaism and I hadn't picked up on any of that yet.' Garrett immediately made the running. He missed the Sex Pistols' appearance at the Lesser Free Trade Hall in Manchester in July 1976 because he was working in Northwich, but after 'Anarchy in the UK' was released in November he embraced punk rock.

Garrett was the first of the pair to find a way to connect with punk culture and he did it by invoking the spirit of Dada, the Bauhaus and Pop in designs of tremendous freshness, energy and wit. His work for the Manchester band Buzzcocks, starting in 1977 while he was still a student, has been eclipsed by Saville's highly publicized output for Factory, but it predates it by a crucial year or two and it adds up to a noteworthy episode in popular culture in its own right. The ribald Dadaist collages Garrett produced in the course of this collaboration still look convincing. His smash-and-grab raids on trashy printed ephemera, lovingly filed away for later use in his scrapbook, have long since become routine among designers, but at the time his anarchically inventive use of both official and demotic sources was new and invigorating. In the early 1980s, during his appropriationist period, Saville repurposed his found material with greater aesthetic precision, but Garrett, already moving on by then, unquestionably did it first.

In 1978, shortly after graduating, Garrett moved to London to work for Andrew Lauder as freelance designer for Radar Records, where Barney Bubbles, Garrett's design hero, was overstretched with work. Soon after arriving, he bumped into Breeden's sister, who told him her brother was working as a cellarman in a casino in Berkeley Square. Garrett asked her to encourage Breeden to call, and when he did Garrett offered him a single sleeve to design – a reissue of 'I Had Too Much to Dream (Last Night)' by the Electric Prunes. It was the first of many covers Breeden designed for bands such as Gang of Four, ABC, Fine Young Cannibals and Scritti Politti. In 1979, Garrett and Breeden moved into a studio in Tottenham Court Road and, in 1984, Garrett and his partner, Kasper de Graaf, suggested that Breeden become a formal partner in their company, Assorted Images. This disturbed Breeden, who had always been wary of anything that smacked of business, and he moved out. He continued designing sleeves until 1996,

New Hormones, montage
by Malcolm Garrett, 1977

when he decided to give it up and concentrate on painting. Today, self-critical as ever, ambitious for his art yet also detached, he is a member of the Royal Society of Portrait Painters, with a studio in the seclusion of the mid-Wales countryside. He readily answers questions about his design days, but reserves his passion for discussions of painterly technique and the achievements of Holbein and Velazquez, Cezanne and Hopper.

It is striking, listening to all their reflections, how true the three of them have remained to the essential aspects of their younger selves. 'I am now a much better version of myself than I was then,' suggests Garrett. 'Peter is a much more accomplished version.' Since leaving St Ambrose, Garrett, like Breeden, has never been back to the school. Saville stayed in touch with David Hancock, who saw their degree show, and in the mid-1990s Saville visited the school at Hancock's request to help an A level student. 'Now Peter had got the charm,' remembers Hancock. 'He'd really got the gift of the gab.' He recalls one occasion when a senior teacher took Saville aside to chastise him for failing to work on his art A level project. 'But about a quarter of an hour later they both came out laughing and joking,' says Hancock. 'Peter Saville had managed to charm him.' It is amusing to learn that Hancock thought both Saville and Garrett did too much copying at school of images and designs they liked and that he told them as much.

From Hancock's point of view, Breeden – 'talented, sensitive, very quiet, almost introverted' – just slipped away. He seemed surprised to learn about his former pupil's current activities as a painter. Garrett and Saville are in no doubt, however, about the subtle, ultimately indefinable influence that Breeden exerted on their early careers. 'He was just so talented,' Garrett enthuses. 'He was brilliant. I so wanted to be as good as Keith.'

NEW EUROPE, NEW SPIRIT?

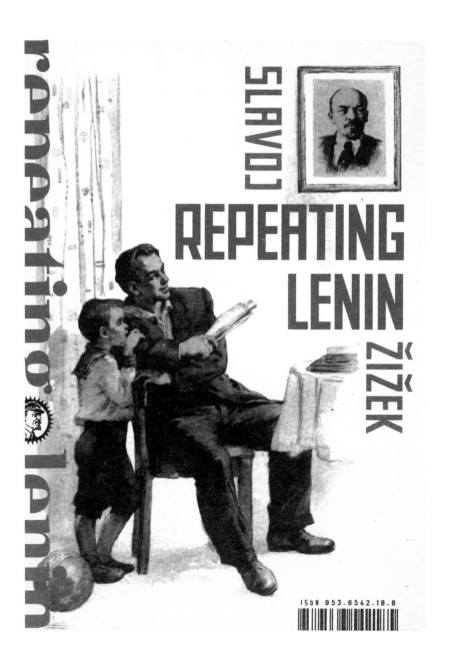

ISbN 953-6542-18-8

Repeating Lenin by Slavoj
Žižek, book cover, Bastard
Books, 2001. Design:
Dejan Krsic and Rutta DD

In central Europe, design is at a crossroads. It is 15 years since the collapse of Communism and the arrival of democracy and the free market, and a great deal has happened in the design communities of countries such as the Czech Republic, Croatia, Slovenia, Poland and Hungary. Design is at different stages of development, reflecting national economic conditions and the relationship of designers with their own local design traditions, but some experiences are shared. There is a chance not simply to produce a local imitation of design in western Europe and America, but to develop goals and ways of working that have their basis in the visual histories and cultural concerns of the region. Without clear thinking and careful planning, it is possible that design in this part of the world could find itself overtaken and corrupted by the worst aspects of design and advertising to the west, where the two activities are becoming inseparable.

My introduction to the region came in 1996 when I was invited by a Hungarian design critic, Krisztina Somogyi, to say a few words at the opening of an exhibition of new digital typography in Pécs in Hungary. I was losing my voice as a result of a throat infection, making it difficult to say anything at all, and this was not inappropriate, perhaps, because the things I found myself wanting to say were not, I imagined, necessarily the things that my Hungarian hosts hoped to hear.

Somogyi, a tireless champion of new design, had done a fine job of gathering work by well-known American and British designers such as the Fuse typeface contributors, The Designers Republic and Why Not Associates, and everything was beautifully displayed in a long, vaulted gallery. Somogyi's aim was to encourage Hungarian designers to embrace new typographic approaches. She was particularly concerned by the poor standard of typography in Hungarian advertising. These western designers were meant to offer examples of new experimental typographic possibilities.

By 1996, though, in western graphic design, events had moved on. The once marginal typographic experiments on display had proved surprisingly successful. Before long, grungy, rule-breaking, legibility-flouting typography was the height of fashion and, for a time, the advertisers loved it. The so-called 'new typography' had become the latest style and a backlash had inevitably followed. Now that I was there in Pécs, I found it hard to endorse a process that seemed likely to end in the same way. What was the point? Why did Hungary need experimental typography generated by cultural and commercial factors specific to countries to its west? Wouldn't it be better to explore graphic and typographic possibilities more closely related to local traditions, developments and requirements, rather than just importing styles that had run their course elsewhere?

My encounter with Hungarian design set the tone, as well as highlighting some enduring issues, for later visits to central Europe. Design scenes such as the one in Prague are small and this creates real communities. The key people all know each other. They feel a sense of shared purpose and have an almost missionary belief in design's potential and importance that one tends not to find these days in places where design is so well established that it is taken for granted. The Czech Typo Design Club, founded in 1996, has just 31 members. In the 1990s, Ales Najbrt of Studio Najbrt, based in a house in a Prague suburb, achieved a position as leader of a new wave of younger designers, who emerged in the post-Communist years, that it would be impossible for any one individual to attain today in London or New York. In terms of its social structure, organizational ambition and commercial development the Prague design scene is similar in size to the design scene in 1960s London. Does that mean Czech designers are 40 years behind British designers? Not at all. For the past decade or more, they have been rapidly making up for lost time. Many of the significant younger figures in central European design travel overseas, and some go abroad to continue their education. They return home with wider perspectives.

The region boasts some excellent designers and here are just a few of them. In the Czech Republic: Studio Najbrt, Robert Novák, Tomás Machek and Petr Babák, Klará Kvízová and Petr Krejzek. In Croatia: Dejan Kršić and Rutta DD, and Studio Cavarpayar. In Slovenia: Slavimir Stojanovic. In Hungary: Zsolt Czakó. Progressive central European designers are struggling to find typographic styles and structures that are both clear and contemporary. In 1999, Dr Iva Janáková, curator at the Museum of Decorative Arts in Prague, observed: 'A lot of Czech graphic design resembles a Tower of Babel, unable to communicate as everything is alike and has nothing to say anyway.'[1] Janáková felt that the confusion of signs, which digital technology had made possible, was the result of a lack of awareness of formal rules and knowledge of the history of design, rather than a deliberate desire for innovation.

Yet it is also clear that the example of the Czech modernist avant-garde of the 1920s and 1930s – its development cut short by the imposition of a repressive Communist government in 1948 – has much to teach Czech designers. Even an occasional visitor can see that the Czech design tradition, visible in Prague's magnificent modernist architecture, has the potential to deliver an invigorating charge to contemporary Czech graphic design and typography, if designers can find a meaningful way of reconnecting with its social idealism and its purifying eye without plunging into postmodern pastiche. The Czech design community is recovering its own history – as can be seen in the pages of the design magazine *Deleatur* co-founded by Janáková and Alan Záruba. The modernist critic and designer Karel Teige has been the subject of considerable scholarship for some years, and in 2003, Janáková curated a superb exhibition in Prague of Czech and American work by Ladislav Sutnar, a modernist innovator of information design.[2]

However, the relationship between modernism and contemporary visual communication is problematic. In recent years, designers around the world have felt drawn towards modernism as a fashionable, contemporary-looking typographic style. A spare, sans serif modernist look has become an all-purpose solution, equally acceptable to pop groups and multinational corporations. Dejan Kršić, writing in Zagreb in 2001, expressed doubts about central European designers' motivations for returning to modernism's repertoire of formal devices: 'Is this "return to modernism" of the 1950s-1960s-1970s only the last in a string of postmodernist pastiches, revivals, neo-styles … or does it really tell us something about the realities of the current situation? … Functionalism deprived of political change and awareness becomes an empty and pointless trend. Today, Modernism is back in vogue, while ideas, idealism and a Utopian way of thinking are not just unpopular, but they are being relegated to the dustbin of history by postmodern cynics.'[3]

This takes us to the heart of the issue. Some of the questions that have arisen again in recent years, in relation to design's role in the advanced capitalist economies of the US or Britain, could seem even more pressing in central Europe. Yet to another way of thinking, they might appear to be completely irrelevant. The complaint, in the wealthy nations, is that communication design has become servile. Its main purpose today is to promote and advertise commercial goods and services, and this is what the vast majority of designers end up doing. It is not that advertising and promotion are wrong in themselves, say design's critics, but the amount of time, talent and resources devoted to this kind of design means that other areas, vital to a healthy, democratic visual culture, are neglected – for instance, information design, design for charitable organizations, design for education, design for cultural purposes.

In the last 20 years, we have educated young designers to believe that this is the way things are, and any sense that designers might once have viewed design differently has faded. One key change is that whereas earlier generations of graphic designers often spoke about their responsibility to society as visual communicators, it is rare to hear designers discuss their role in such terms today. 'The main questions that must now be addressed to designers themselves are how do you view your role?' writes Kršić. 'How do you perceive it? Not what kind of work would you like to do, but what is it that you want to achieve through it?'4

Western designers are, however, in a privileged position. They live in secure, stable, wealthy societies. The need for design is now well established and a broad range of clients has the money to engage their services. National economies experience fluctuations, but there is plenty of design work to go around. Even radicals make their criticisms from a position of relative security. Critics of capitalist design tend to occupy a position on the political left, but there is no prospect in western Europe of a dramatic political swing in this direction, and this is even more improbable in the US.

The situation in central Europe could not be more different. For these societies, the period after Communism was insecure and unstable. Yugoslavia was ravaged by war. The very capitalism that western discontents deplore offered hope of liberation from decades of restriction under Communism. The free market promised freedom in every sense. Any critique based on the idea of a move back towards socialism could strike those who have experienced life under its heel as a bad joke. Nevertheless, while the official line is that capitalism will make everything better, the reality is that many struggle to survive. On my visits to central Europe, people pointed out some of the ways in which their lives are less good today than they were under Communism. There is pocket-lining political corruption, new extremes of inequality between those profiting from post-Communist chaos and ordinary people, a less equitable deal for women and dwindling state support, in a new survival-of-the-fittest culture, for the arts. The negative aspects of rampant commercialism can be seen in Prague's spoilt historic centre. Those who live there and loved the city as it was feel distaste and dismay at this sorry spectacle.

Still, designers must deal with the circumstances they find themselves in. The understandable priority has been to find work and, as a vital part of that process, to make the case for design to potential clients and the public. Kršić describes how British type-designer Jonathan Barnbrook told an audience in Zagreb that he had rejected Nike as a client and would not do work for Coca-Cola. This degree of fastidiousness must have astonished Croatian designers who, in Kršić's view, would jump at the chance to take on such large commissions from high-paying companies.

In Prague, Ales Najbrt has fared better than most, working for Altron, an energy supplier, and Agropol, an agriculture conglomerate, but Najbrt underlines the problem of finding sophisticated clients – even today. 'Under communism,' he told *Print*, 'nothing evolved.'[5] Many clients have little sense of how a design programme might be implemented consistently across their businesses, or what they might have to gain commercially from a well-coordinated visual identity. This is an inevitable problem in any emerging design economy and designers throughout the region are learning to deal with it.

Lana Cavar of Studio Cavarpayar in Zagreb notes how it became clear at the end of the 1990s, when the Croatian Designer Association held its first exhibition, that the clients of Croatian designers tended to be non-profit organizations, cultural organizations, smaller companies, theatres and small publishers. Only a limited number of designers had managed to win clients in the state and business sectors that might make a substantial impact on the Croatian economy. To help to forge these connections, the association has been working towards the establishment of a design centre. Its primary task, explains Cavar, 'would be to establish deeper contacts and cooperation with state structures, potential clients and the society in general, to conceive and realize projects that would help educate people on [the] advantages and possibilities of investing in design and make the state structures, economy and culture understand and use design as a means of development and practical transformation of their everyday business.'[6]

It is interesting to hear a young designer, who produces highly contemporary work, talk about design in these terms. In Britain, it would be unusual for a designer of the same age, working for similar clients, to express such a hope. Britain's Design Council was founded long ago to take care of these matters. Economic prosperity and a flourishing design scene mean that young designers simply don't have to worry about such fundamental concerns. The system will run without them, and design long ago split into two largely separate worlds. Business-minded, wealth-creating design, operating at national and international levels, is undertaken by big, unglamorous design consultancies, with many designers on their payrolls. This sector has become so highly professionalized in the last 25 years that there is not much space for small, creatively driven studios to become involved in these projects, even if they wanted to do so.

In central Europe, the stakes are different. Economic growth is a priority and young designers are in the same campaigning position, when it comes to the benefits of design for business and society, as earlier generations of British or American designers. They are almost duty-bound to think more closely about their social role and what they want to achieve than their sometimes rather complacent colleagues in western design. There is a real danger, too, that if designers don't rise to meet the challenge, western design conglomerates will grab the major projects. 'We expect big brand agencies will come to Prague,' says Najbrt, 'and we need to be a competitor for them.'[7] These agencies are already arriving. Euro RSCG Prague sits like a gun emplacement on a hill overlooking the city. Its mission statement is given in ringing phrases, in Czech and English, on the front of the building: 'Euro RSCG Prague is the first multi-site integrated agency, covering all communication disciplines, with over 1,000 talents in 14 cities in the New Europe: Belgrade, Bratislava, Bucharest, Budapest, Kiev, Ljubljana, Moscow, Prague, Riga, Sofia, Tallin, Vilnius, Warsaw, Zagreb. Because today marketers need more than good advertising and promotion, Euro RSCG Prague aims to develop Creative Business Ideas® that apply to their business strategy in new ways to drive profitable growth.'

I hope that Najbrt and other committed, adventurous designers in Prague, Zagreb, Ljubljana, Warsaw, Budapest and elsewhere can hold their ground. In the west, design's position is probably now fixed. It has had its formative years, its infancy and adolescence. It has achieved some kind of maturity and the visual culture we observe around us today is the way it turned out. Central European designers are right to look at the west to see what they might learn, especially about design as a business, but they should do so in a critical spirit. Who says we got it right? Is western design and, for that matter, western society every-thing it could be? What works and what doesn't work? What could be improved? If there are aspects of western design that seem miscon-ceived and mistaken, then why rush to repeat those mistakes? Why duplicate western models in every detail, when they may not be appro-priate to local customs, concerns and needs? And why surrender to the cynical, emasculating, postmodern malaise, especially at a time when many in the west are challenging this?

In the 1930s, Prague was one of the most industrially and cultural-ly sophisticated cities in the world. What might be possible if designers were to take the idealistic, perhaps rather utopian view that design might be applied, as the modernists once dreamed, in the cause of a more just, equitable, functional, beautiful and better-run society? If designers decline to take responsibility for the quality of the visual environment in which everyone lives and works, then whose task can it possibly be? Where is an enlightened approach to design going to come from, if not from people with an educated knowledge of design?

New European designers are full of energy. They believe in themselves and know what they want to do. They are obviously having a good time. They are inspired. The situation is still fluid, with the possibility of great developments as well as wrong turnings, and this is exciting – for onlookers as well as participants. You cannot visit the region without feeling this new spirit and sense of possibility and, in the last few years, most of the designers mentioned here have been written about in American, French, British and Chinese magazines. That is certainly a sign that their work is arousing interest, although it is too early to say in what ways influences from central Europe might be felt in the west. The crucial thing is that designers in the Czech Republic, Slovakia, Slovenia, Croatia, Poland, Hungary and their neighbours should believe in the creative and organizational possibilities of this new spirit. It is their visual environment they are shaping, in their own way, for their own populations.

Perhaps the most valuable lesson would be for central European designers to resist the western brand-mania that leads to everything looking the same in the shops, streets and media, and assert the human value of local visual traditions. Finding a way to reconcile these concerns with the urgent demands of economic progress, while preserving a sense of national identity, may be their most challenging design task.

WRITING WITH PICTURES

W.G. Sebald, who died in a car crash in 2001, is one of the greatest European writers of recent years. His books *Vertigo* (1990), *The Emigrants* (1993), *The Rings of Saturn* (1995) and *Austerlitz* (2001), all first published in German, defy easy categorization. They have been summarized as part hybrid fiction, part memoir and part travelogue, while the adjectives most frequently used to describe their extraordinary prose style, built on long, elegant sentences, are 'haunting' and 'mesmeric'. These four books affected me more deeply than anything I have read in a long time. I share the view of many Sebald readers that *Austerlitz* is a masterwork, a book so good that you find yourself constantly rereading passages to savour the luminous intensity with which he evokes people encountered, places visited, things seen and atmospheres recalled.

Sebald is brilliantly visual. He makes you realize with some discomfort that you often fail to look attentively enough at what you see. Another novelist referred to the 'phenomenal configuration' of the author's mind, and what astonishes and delights in Sebald's sentences, superbly rendered by his translators, is his ability to convey not just the detail of so many things hitting the senses in a rain of fleeting simultaneous impressions, but the precise emotional shading and personal import of each of these moments. His eye records with photographic accuracy and then these perceptions are recovered from memory and reconstituted as fictional experience with the same exhilaratingly scrupulous fidelity. The complication in Sebald's writing, which he apparently intended, lies in our uncertainty about how much of what he describes derives from his own experiences (seemingly a lot) and how much of it is largely or entirely imagined. On a reading of the books alone, the narrators show every sign of being Sebald himself, but we know from what he has said elsewhere that these melancholy figures are fictionalized versions of the author.

Another striking aspect of the books is the use Sebald makes of photographs and other visual material, such as architectural plans, engravings, paintings and restaurant bills. He drops these uncaptioned images into the text, providing an additional level of documentary 'evidence', and you become convinced that Sebald really must have undertaken the walk or visited the building that his narrator describes. Literary reviewers usually note the presence of these images, acknowledging that they add to the books' unique flavour, but the role of such material in the composition of the texts and the exact ways in which text and images relate to each other have received little attention. This is not something that reviewers usually have to consider since few literary writers work in this way. John Berger, beginning with *A Fortunate Man* (1967), using photographs by his friend Jean Mohr, is one of the most notable. Geoff Dyer's *The Missing of the Somme* (1994), a book about war and remembrance, also Sebald's themes, has elements of this approach.

If *Austerlitz* is Sebald's most sophisticated marriage of writing and imagery, its use of images also raises the most questions because, of all the books, it is the one most like a work of fiction, though of a highly unconventional kind. In 1939, not yet five, Jacques Austerlitz is sent to Britain on a *Kindertransport* and placed with foster-parents in Wales. Never happy, he excels at school and becomes an architectural historian. He is told nothing about his identity and it is years before he even learns his original name. Later, the past he has always avoided thinking about returns to haunt him and he goes in search of his lost parents. He relates this story in a series of sometimes coincidental meetings with the book's narrator, who reports it to us. (Everything in Sebald is indirect. The narrator no more witnessed these events than we did.) British and American editions of Austerlitz show a photograph on the cover of a young boy dressed like a cavalier, and our assumption that this must be Austerlitz proves correct. Yet, clearly, if Austerlitz is a fictional character, the picture must be of someone else. The status of many images in the book becomes equally questionable. In fact, the cover photograph is a boyhood picture of a real architectural historian, one of Sebald's friends. Austerlitz is known to be a composite of several real people.

Austerlitz is always taking photographs and he entrusts his collection, which 'one day would be all that was left of his life', to the narrator, who uses them to assemble his story. After Austerlitz has a breakdown, some of his photographs play a therapeutic role, helping him to reconstruct his 'buried experiences'. The book's entire sequence of 87 images in 415 pages (Penguin UK edition) can be seen to serve a similar purpose. Here, more than ever, it seems clear that the images have not simply arrived after the writing was finished, to be used as 'illustrations'. Sebald employs them as a way of generating, one might even say designing, the meandering narrative. In one of the book's most remarked-upon uses of photography, the text stops and Sebald shows a sequence of four doorways in Terezín, about 64 kilometres (40 miles) from Prague and site of a Jewish ghetto in the Second World War, which Austerlitz visits. The brutal last door, with its heavy iron bands, cannot fail to suggest a death-camp gas chamber, although no such thing is stated in the text.

The question of page design arises here. In a rare essay about the visual aspect of Sebald's books, Robin Kinross criticizes the crudity of design and production in the Harvill editions that introduced Sebald in Britain.[1] Kinross notes that in *The Rings of Saturn* some of the images have moved from their positions in the original German edition published by the Andere Bibliothek. What is not clear, however, is the extent to which Sebald was involved in the placement of these images in the original or subsequent editions. He is known to have been highly involved in the revision of his translations into English and French, so it seems unlikely, given the importance of the pictures, that he would have wanted no say in the matter. Like Austerlitz, he was a devoted photographer. 'In school I was in the dark room all the time,' he told an interviewer, 'and I've always collected stray photographs; there's a great deal of memory in them.'[2] He carried a small camera and was constantly on the lookout for old photos, postcards and newspaper cuttings. An obituary noted: 'He was an exacting customer at the University of East Anglia copy shop, discussing what might be done with his images, adjusting the size and contrast.'[3] In the earlier books, the degraded, photocopied look of some of the pictures seems to have been a deliberate effect.

The Penguin design of *Austerlitz* shows a marked improvement on the Harvill volumes. The book takes the form of an almost continuous paragraph. One stupendous sentence unwinds over 11 pages, but the text is made much less overwhelming than this might sound by a narrow measure, generous line-spacing and ample margins. The pictures relate to this text area much more carefully than in the earlier English translations. The last three Terezín doors fill the height of the text column and all are cropped to the same narrow width – by Sebald? – like a series of tombstones. They become bleak and moving portents of the fate of Austerlitz's family.

At one point, in a reverie, Austerlitz recalls the window displays of the Antikos Bazar, an antique shop on the west side of the town square in Terezín, where he had waited, hoping that someone would arrive to open the shop. Sebald shows a photograph of what he calls this 'curious emporium' and the narrator describes the seemingly haphazard but, for him, highly mysterious and meaningful displays in the Bazar's windows. This is illustrated with two more photographs.

Since I read this passage, my thoughts have sometimes returned to the Antikos Bazar. In 2004, I was in Prague, attending a conference, and it occurred to me that, if the shop existed where Sebald said it was, I now had the opportunity to see it for myself.

Shop window, Terezín, 2004. Photograph: Rick Poynor

93 Writing with pictures

So, on a Saturday morning, I caught the bus from Prague to Terezín to find out how closely Sebald's description of the town compared with reality. After travelling through the countryside for about an hour we pulled into the town square, and there, tucked away behind a fringe of trees on the far side, was the Antikos Bazar.

The façade was in most respects the same as the one shown across two pages in Sebald's book, but inevitably, after so long, the objects displayed in the four windows had changed. There was no sign that day of the three brass mortars 'which had about them the suggestion of an oracular utterance', of the 'endless landscape painted around a lampshade in fine brush-strokes', or of the moth-eaten stuffed squirrel 'forever perched in the same position'.[4] Remembering Austerlitz, with his face pressed against the glass, I lingered outside the Bazar, examining the swordsticks, hunting knives, military uniforms, field telephones, empty beer bottles, antlers, porcelain teacups, crystal decanters, nude figurines and three waxy fish heads mounted on a wooden board that now filled the windows. Just as Sebald had described, at 11 o'clock in the morning the place was closed, making it impossible to explore the treasure trove of fishing rods, old wooden skis and bedpans that could be glimpsed in its deep, shadowy recesses through windows misted with condensation.

In other respects, Terezín was different from the book. It is raining when Austerlitz visits and he describes an oppressive, uncannily deserted town where he sees hardly anyone the entire time he is there apart from a man who is mentally disturbed. On the day I visited, people were on the move in the streets, though there was hardly any traffic and Terezín preserved a stillness that even the sound of techno music pounding from a battered car parked across the road from the Antikos Bazar could not dispel. Austerlitz records that the Bazar is the only shop of any kind except for a tiny grocery store. This intensifies the inaccessible emporium's air of strangeness. Why is it there if it is rarely open for business and there are no customers? There are other shops nearby and it seems unlikely, given the size of the town, that there were only two shops when Sebald passed through. To a visitor's eyes, however, these shops also possess an air of mystery, their façades painted with the same intense yellows, pinks and greens as the grand buildings in the square, their shopfront typography angular and strange.

Another thing I noticed, as I wandered around, was that the windows of these shops selling provisions presented the same kind of randomly organized tableaux of disparate things as the Antikos Bazar's

Doorway, Terezín, 2004.
Photograph: Rick Poynor

windows. The packages and containers on display brushed together behind the glass to suggest elusive kinds of significance and meaning, endowing ordinary household items with a heightened presence and a peculiar fascination. These whimsical, three-dimensional constructions, which might almost have been artworks, betrayed an element of uninhibited expression that exceeded the requirements of commerce and conveyed a surprising degree of warmth.

I had to move into the cobblestoned side streets around Terezín's town square to experience something closer to the mood of desertion that Sebald evokes. The plaster cladding along the lower parts of some of the walls has dropped off in great chunks, exposing the raw brickwork-like skin torn from the surface of a wound. Someone told me later that this was caused by the floods of 2002, which damaged Terezín as well as Prague, so the town must look more desolate now than it did when Sebald visited. Sebald has Austerlitz dwell at some length on the gates and doorways of Terezín, finding them the most uncanny aspect of the town – 'all of them,' he writes, 'obstructing access to a darkness never yet penetrated, a darkness in which I thought … there was no more movement at all'.[5] He shows a series of haunting pictures of these apertures, and it is true that they do seem to be shut with a kind of brutal finality, sealing off whatever secrets they might hide, just like the Bazar does.

In Sebald's novel, Austerlitz visits the Ghetto Museum (though not the nearby Small Fortress used by the Gestapo as a prison) and spends a long time looking at exhibits that document in overwhelming detail the lives of the ghetto's Jewish prisoners and the history of their persecution. Emerging from the museum, he imagines that 60,000 people had never been taken away and are still living in the ghetto, crammed into the basements and attics, 'a silent assembly, filling the entire space occupied by the air, hatched with grey as it was by the fine rain'.[6] As I climb aboard the bus to return to Prague, the weather takes a turn for the worse and the first drops of rain start to fall.

TECHNOLOGY IN EVERYDAY LIFE

For years now museums have been in love with the idea of interactivity. Curators fear that for many potential visitors objects held in static positions behind glass are boring. People want to be involved and the younger the museum-goer, the more likely this is to be the case. Children like pressing buttons, turning handles and watching screens. They want to see balls rolling along grooves and waves sloshing in tanks as a result of their efforts. Families seek entertainment and an enjoyable day out. The curatorial purpose of these displays is to educate and museums hope that by sugaring the pill visitors will want to linger and learn.

Yet one of the pleasures of museum going has always been the chance to look closely at unfamiliar objects. This process, too, is 'interactive', though it is slower, quieter and more contemplative. It requires a willingness to move patiently from object to object, trying to appreciate what each one was for and how it was used and to take the time to compare similar types of exhibit. The Pitt Rivers Museum in Oxford offers one of the most remarkable experiences of this kind in Britain, its Victorian glass cabinets crammed with displays of archaeological and ethnographic artefacts from every corner of the globe: baskets, pottery, jewellery, masks, amulets, tools, weapons, locks and keys, musical instruments, figure carvings and nail fetishes.

Where most museums edit their collections to show only the most important or artistically accomplished exhibits, at Pitt Rivers it is as though the storage cupboards have turned transparent, allowing an unrestricted view of their entire contents. The competitive profusion of objects – more than the casual visitor can absorb without many visits – makes the museum a place of wonder, an inexhaustibly vivid record of the diversity of human imagination and invention.

The Science Museum in London has many galleries devoted to the interactive approach, but its 'Making the Modern World' gallery, which opened in 2000, trusts in the power of exceptional objects to captivate the viewer. The main gallery has some spectacular pieces: Stephenson's Rocket, a Ford Model T, a Lockheed Electra airliner, a German V2 flying bomb. Exhibits like these are so imposing that it would be possible to walk through the main gallery without noticing the five glass-fronted displays telling the story of 'Technology in Everyday Life' from 1750 to 2000 that occupy the length of the north-ern wall. Yet these displays, assembled with the same curatorial inclusiveness that makes Pitt Rivers so spellbinding, are brilliantly realized. It is hard to imagine a more absorbing array of manufactured artefacts. The Museum of Modern Art's refurbished design galleries don't even come close. 'Making the Modern World' is not a design gallery, but invention and design are inextricably linked so the dis-plays can be savoured not only for what they tell us about the uses of technology, but for what they reveal about the evolution of form.

Each of the seven-metre wide displays contains between 150 and 300 items, roughly spanning the periods 1750-1820, 1820-1880, 1880-1939, 1939-1968 and 1968-2000. The smaller objects are arranged in groups on plain, step-like shelves; larger exhibits stand at the back or to the side; some items hang on wires from the ceiling.[1] A clever rationale underpins the groupings in each section: the curators employ classification systems devised at the time. The layout of the first display derives from the *Encyclopédie* (1751-80) by Denis Diderot and Jean d'Alembert, which makes use of three kinds of classification: memory, covering manufacturing trades and natural history; reason, covering sciences, medicine, language, philosophy; and imagination, covering music, poetry, literature, the arts. In much the same way, the fourth display (1939-1968) is based on the 1951 Festival of Britain's division into five areas: art, architecture, science, technology and industrial design, each section then subdivided into themes such as 'power and production' and 'homes and gardens'. The final display takes its cue from Stewart Brand's book, *The Next Whole Earth*

Technology in Everyday Life, detail of display for 1880-1939, Science Museum, London, 2000. Graphic design: Farrow Design. Photograph: Fredrika Lökholm

Catalog (1980), which is divided into nine sections, including craft, community, learning, soft technology and politics.

While the conceptual framework that structures the displays is exemplary, it is often the unexpected juxtapositions generated by these methods of classification that engage the viewer. 'Beautiful as the chance encounter of a sewing machine and an umbrella on a dissecting table,' wrote the French poet Lautréamont, and his words became a popular maxim for the Surrealists. The display placements possess this quality of almost uncanny aptness. In the third section (1880-1939) there is a collection of medical artefacts spread over two shelves. This includes a door plate that once belonged to Le Docteur P. F. Gachet, Van Gogh's physician; a wheel-shaped guide to the shade of false teeth – one of the 24 teeth-spokes is missing; a brass pill-coating contraption; a pneumothorax device to collapse the lungs of tuberculosis patients to rest them; a prosthetic arm with a fork attached to the hand; and a set of hypodermic syringes in a dull grey metal case with rounded corners engraved with the name of Frederick Treves Esq., surgeon to Joseph Merrick, the Elephant Man, whose story was filmed in 1980 by David Lynch. The pieces fit together in their group to form a still life that serves its curatorial purpose by showing the varieties of implement used at this time by medical people, while also offering a concentrated experience of 'object-ness' and the mysterious quiddity of things that is much harder to quantify. The elaborate precision of the object groups, where each numbered item fits into the space provided for it like an element in a jigsaw, gives these collections-in-miniature a peculiar resonance.

The further back you go in time, the stranger some of these objects become. The first display boasts silver tongue-scrapers, a long-handled bullet extractor for delving into wounds, a 'chamber horse' with a seat like a big black bellows said to provide the same exercise as horse-riding, and *memento mori* rings and broaches; the second has a clockwork enema syringe; the third a package containing a corrective cap made from ribbon, elastic and net to flatten the ears. A grinning girl wears it on the box – 'It's comfy'. It is not that any of these needs has gone away. We are still scraping our furry tongues, repairing the damage caused by firearms, purging our innards of toxins, using exercise machines to make us fitter, worrying about protuberant ears, and reminding ourselves that all things must pass, but the tools have been assimilated, normalized and refined. Awkward early devices were superseded by shapelier, less eccentric, more effective versions, or people found other outlets and remedies.

The many objects relating to the history of electricity follow the same upward climb from eccentricity to normality. The first section, before 1820, shows a crepuscular, non-electric world. In 1831, Faraday discovered the dynamo, which allowed the generation of a continuous current. The use of electricity for a wide variety of medical purposes soon followed. The second display features a Magneto-electric machine manufactured in 1862 for the treatment of nervous diseases, a lockable wooden box with a large magnet inside, a handle to turn a series of cogs, and two wires attached at either end for delivering the current. By 1925, the idea of electric revivification had become a fairground attraction. For the price of a penny, dropped into a slot on the Electric Tonic machine – 'Keep fit. Use often', a slogan advises – you could administer yourself with harmless but supposedly refreshing ripples of electricity. Yet electric power directed at the right target does possess the near magical ability to animate quiescent flesh and restore life itself. In the section about the contemporary world, there is a battery-operated defibrilator, Type 180C, made around 1975 by Cardiac Recorders, used to restart the heart after a heart attack with a short, high-voltage pulse of electricity. At the top of the plain red box it says 'Resuscitation Unit' and the control panel on the front is covered with knobs, switches, operating instructions and plug-in leads that connect to large round electrodes: 'Apply electrodes firmly to chest and press trigger button.' All these details make it obvious what the device is for, if we haven't already seen one on countless TV shows set in casualty departments and emergency rooms, but its bland, generic box shape says nothing specific about how or where it will be applied, or about the power it contains. It looks no different in essence from the yellow plastic unit with a carrying handle, used for testing portable electrical appliances, displayed a little further along the same shelf.

By the late twentieth century, many objects give little clue as to their functions. Even though we know it already, this is one of the notable aspects of travelling along the timeline of 250 years of technology and taking the measure of hundreds of everyday artefacts. The object world of the late eighteenth century, seen in the first display, has a heaviness and density that seems oppressive to a twenty-first-century eye accustomed to dazzling colours and delicacy of form. Two-hundred-year-old things are often bulky, elementary in shape and brutally real. They are almost all the same colour, dark brown, because so many of them are made of wood or iron. Tools, hourglasses, tobacco jars, iron chests, medicine chests, door locks, spinning wheels, horse measuring sticks, truncheons, flintlock pistols, whips for punishing slaves – everything is brown. What colour there was would have come from fabrics (not part of the display) and ceramics, though the muted earthenware plates on show do little to lift the mood. By the Victorian period, the wood is lighter in colour and warmer in tone, but the world of manufactured objects is still largely brown and, in the age of heroic advances in engineering, forms remain ponderous and heavy. A studio camera, made out of wood by Charles G. Collins around 1870, resembles a piece of furniture. At this point there is no other material from which to construct it. This specimen, used for portraits, has no shutter; its lens cap controlled the length of exposure. Cameras, a new industrial archetype, had not yet developed to the point where they had acquired their own characteristic lines and shapes, or as we might say today, product semantics.

By the fourth display, focused on the middle decades of the twentieth century, we are in a different world. Everything is less substantial now, smaller and lighter. There is much less sense of *matter*. Objects are far more likely to be made of synthetics than wood. There are new materials such as nylon and Formica and everything has a colour. People have more to spend and trademarks and brand names proliferate: Dunhill cigarettes, Quink ink, Castrol motor oil, Sunsilk shampoo, SR toothpaste, Watneys Red Barrel, Littlewoods football pools. Electricity has enabled the creation of a huge array of new products: radio, television, vacuum cleaners, washing machines, food blenders, power tools, rotary mowers, electric typewriters, tape recorders and cine projectors. Within decades, these technological wonders were joined by synthesizers, videocassette recorders, personal stereos, mobile phones, satellite TV receivers, radar speed-trap cameras, kidney dialysis machines, ultrasound scanning equipment, and credit card terminals. As design theorist John Chris Jones has noted, this is a non-mechanical age that depends on 'electric power, low currents, complex circuits, minute components, invisible processes, relativities (in place of absolute standards), and on finding external analogues and processes fast and delicate enough to be matched to the operations of the eye, the ear, the brain or any other organ of the body.'[2] In a flexible computer keyboard produced in 1999, a formerly hard-bodied object with moving parts, made familiar by many generations of the typewriter, becomes a seamless, malleable, touch-sensitive work-pad. How to show Microsoft Windows (1992) without running it on a screen? Here, the packaging and logo has to stand for a product that exists as immaterial digital code.

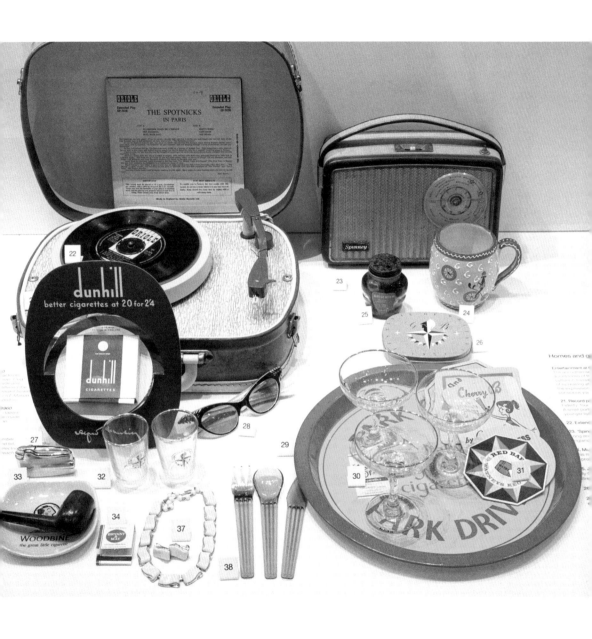

Technology in Everyday Life, detail of display for 1939-1968, Science Museum, London, 2000. Graphic design: Farrow Design. Photograph: Fredrika Lökholm

In the last of the five displays, the tendency towards lightness, slightness and transience is even more advanced. Wood is reserved mainly for making furniture today. For everyday technology, plastic in bright shades of yellow, orange, red and blue has taken its place. Where this would be too much for continuous daily use, indifferent beiges and greys have become the new brown. Many objects feel as insubstantial, as gossamer thin, as the sure-fit, safe play and ultra-strong condoms in wallets splashed with gaudy graphics, and as throwaway as the pack of Pampers disposable nappies that sits next to them – and some are just tacky. Products are well made, in the sense that they will do their job effectively, but compared with many earlier artefacts, they no longer look well crafted. These mass-produced items lack the gravitas bestowed by a shaping hand and, judged in formal terms, they are inarticulate and dull. If it is true that we shape our tools and then our tools shape us, as McLuhan said, then it is natural to wonder what effect such inconsequential artefacts will have on their users. The weightiness of objects produced during the industrial revolution suggests certainty and purpose. Eighteenth-century steel tools such as pincers, vices, compasses and hacksaws resembled weapons or implements for inflicting punishment and correction. There were fewer manufactured objects then and their owners would have valued these possessions highly as sources of livelihood and as indicators of social status, craft knowledge and skill. Merely lifting the tools would have required strong hands and a sure grasp. We have thousands more things now and they are easily come by and discarded. It is doubtful that many of our technological objects matter to us as much. We care more about the 'invisible processes' they enable than about their material presence and form.

In the course of researching this essay, I visited 'Making the Modern World' on five occasions, each time spending a couple of hours in the gallery. Sometimes I drifted between the displays, allow-ing whim and chance to determine what I would look at next; some-times I moved back and forth with more purpose, comparing similar pieces from different periods or trying to establish links. I made no attempt to be systematic by starting at the first object in a display and working through in numerical sequence, though this would have been one way to ensure I looked at everything. No one approaches museum exhibits in this fashion, though, and my interest was in any case in groups of objects. If an arrangement happened to catch my eye, I would study the individual pieces. I was still discovering new items after three or four visits and even now there are plenty I have not examined closely. If we assume that there are 1,000 exhibits, then at a brisk one minute per item it would take more than 16 hours to peruse every object and caption. Many visitors sample the five displays in a matter of minutes. People tend to be most attracted by artefacts they remember from earlier in their lives and they comment on them to their companions. On one visit, a woman noticed me crouching down examining Frederick Treves's syringes and stopped to take a look. She attracted the attention of a teenage girl who was filling out an educational questionnaire and dictated to her the spelling of Merrick and Treves. The girl wrote this down without pausing to look at the object and went away.

Although the displays are not intended to be read as art, these still life combinations and clusters possess great suggestive power and they evoke the same kinds of emotion, association and recollection as art. Many of the objects can be appreciated in aesthetic terms and the visual relationships established between them within each group add another layer of aesthetic interest. A display of disparate objects can be viewed as a kind of assemblage or collage and artists, recognizing the fascination of both random conjunctions and things organized in series, often employ forms of taxonomy and presentation derived from museum practice in their work. I have never seen another sequence of exhibits concerned with technology that contrives such a complex interplay of objects.

The Science Museum staff created full-size replicas of the displays at the museum's storage building in London and used the mock-ups to try out ideas and arrangements until they were satisfied. 'The greater prominence of history within the Science Museum's displays over the last decade, with galleries such as … *Making the Modern World*, is the product of a determined and unashamed reorientation of the museum's Collections Division towards historical scholarship as the appropriate mode of engagement with the collections which we curate,' writes Dr Timothy Boon, deputy director of the project at the Science Museum.[3] Boon notes that at a time when people experience the world virtually, through the PC, 'the real thing in the specific place gains an enhanced cultural value'.[4] The 'Technology in Everyday Life' display exceeds the casual visitor's grasp on a single visit and is probably best experienced and absorbed in focused bursts as a research need or interest arises. It asks viewers to open their senses, look hard, use their imaginations and allow these endlessly diverse, ingenious and life-improving objects to tell their innumerable stories.

LOOK INWARD, AUSTRALIA

Seen from afar, Australia has always been an unknown territory when it comes to graphic design. Few Australian names are well known outside the country. Older designers may be familiar with figures such as Ken Cato, Garry Emery and Barrie Tucker, but no younger graphic designers have had the kind of international impact that Marc Newson made on furniture, or Baz Luhrman on art direction for film. In the last decade, few Australian designers have promoted themselves beyond the country's shores. Stephen Banham, typographer and self-publisher, is a striking exception. Mambo, with one of the most original graphic identities of any clothing company anywhere, has received little attention in the design press. Designers invited to lecture in Australia often seemed to return with the view that little was happening down under.

In recent years, Australia has emerged as a vibrant contributor to international culture at all levels, with an impact relative to its small population (19 million) that other countries might envy. Australian actors and musicians seem to be everywhere. Australian architecture is stunningly inventive; one of the country's finest architects, Glenn Murcutt, won the prestigious Pritzker Prize in 2002. Australian writers such as Tim Winton and Peter Carey, awarded the Booker Prize in 2001, are held in high regard. Australian film-makers continue to produce some impressive films; recent examples include *Lantana*, *Rabbit-Proof*

Fence and *Japanese Story*. As Australians never hesitate to tell you, their cuisine is world class and standards of hospitality are high. Australia today is an exciting, energetic, hugely stimulating place to visit. Its globally acclaimed staging of the Olympics in 2000 did much to boost national self-belief.

Graphic design is not untouched by this sense of energy and conviction and in the past few years there have been some notable developments. To understand Australian design's position now, though, it is necessary to consider how it has developed. Australian practitioners have always measured themselves against what was happening abroad and from the 1930s to the 1960s – and beyond – many would seek work experience overseas. The American designer Les Mason, a former sailor and bar owner, who arrived in Melbourne in 1961, was a key figure. 'He was the most informed person that I'd come across,' recalls Garry Emery, 'and he was the one that really built bridges for me, made design legible so that I could grasp the social connections.'

Mason was steeped in ideas about type and spatial organization brought to the US by the European émigrés. He had read György Kepes's *The Language of Vision* (1944) and the book was a decisive early influence on Emery, too. The young Australian's other sources included Danish and Scandinavian modernism – seen in furniture and homewares – Karl Gerstner's *Designing Programmes* (1963) and European modernists such as Max Bill and Josef Müller-Brockmann.[1] Then came Push Pin and Herb Lubalin. As Emery describes it, Australia in the 1960s and 1970s was not an easy place to be a designer: it was a self-conscious, laconic, masculine society, shaped by its convict origins and deeply suspicious of anything perceived as intellectual or highbrow. 'I believe that's very much part of the Australian psyche,' he says. 'It's a kind of distrust. Maybe it's not so visible now, but it's not so long ago that it was highly visible.' Design was a 'cissy's game' that Emery would only ever discuss with fellow designers and he thinks this anti-intellectualism persists even today. The Australian belief in an egalitarian society goes back to its earliest days and 'tall poppies', people who try to stand out above the crowd, have to be lopped to restore equality. This distaste for the 'self-promotion caper', as a Sydney-based designer described it to me, is perhaps one reason why Australian designers have tended to be overlooked.

Another result of Australian design's tendency to underplay itself is that there are surprisingly few sources of information about it. Geoffrey Caban's *A Fine Line: A History of Australian Commercial Art* is the only detailed general study; it is long out of print and nothing comparable has since appeared.[2] Even more crucially, Australian graphic design has lacked a vigorous, well-established design press to report on its activities, analyse developments, encourage debate and reflect its sense of identity, though there are signs that this could change. In June 2001, *Desktop* magazine abandoned its focus on technology to concentrate on new developments in design; a size change and a lively redesign reflected its new direction. Nigel Beechy, president of the New South Wales branch of the Australian Graphic Design Association (AGDA), believes there is a pressing need to improve the quantity and quality of design discussion. 'A lot of design writing – and there isn't a lot – tends to have almost a pop star mentality, going for the cool, groovy designers of the moment.'

AGDA, founded in 1988 and staffed by enthusiastic volunteers, has undoubtedly made a significant contribution to the development of Australian design. It has a voluminous website, organizes lectures and holds national awards every two years. But it still has its critics. James de Vries of De Luxe, a Sydney studio specializing in editorial design work, doesn't view AGDA as sufficiently representative. 'It's been a bit of a coterie of like-minded people who entertain each other,' he says, 'a very small segment of the industry.' Graeme Smith, co-founder of Precinct, a medium-sized Sydney studio, suggests that AGDA's focus on issues is too narrow. 'For instance, they are forever talking about free pitching and the craft of graphic design and how clients need to be educated, but I think that's just facile,' he says. 'It's not the client that needs to be educated. It's the whole culture.'

Smith argues that design in Australia is still a special case – luxury items for the affluent, rather than well-designed things for everyone, which are part of the fabric of everyday life. Some areas of Australian life certainly do seem to be less 'designed' than others. Restaurants are often fabulous and wine labels are a minor art form, but supermarket design and food packaging, and retail design in general, are much less sophisticated. 'In Britain, I'd say that generally the public is very well educated as to what design is,' says Dean Hastie, a British designer who arrived in Australia in 1990 and co-founded the design company Nova in Sydney. 'You walk into a supermarket and everything is designed to within an inch of its life and it's the norm. But here it's not.' Others see it differently. '[Australians] have a much greater awareness of what good design is now, spreading through the echelons of the community, even down to your mums and dads at home,' says Penny Bowring, managing director of Emery Vincent Design. 'They are being fed better design and accepting it, which we always said they would.'

ART
&
DESIGN

Faculty of Art and Design

Sign for Monash
University, Melbourne,
1999. Design:
Garry Emery Design

Any design-aware visitor to Australia will inevitably ask whether there are, or have been, characteristic and immediately recognizable national forms of graphic design. In *A Fine Line*, the Australian designer Arthur Leydin, talking about the 1950s, argues that Australian design should be assessed from a regional point of view and not in comparison with what was being done in Europe or the US. 'Australian designers,' he observes, 'could only answer the cultural demands of the society of which they were a part.'[3] There have been periodic attempts to isolate and celebrate aspects of a specifically Australian graphic tradition. In 1980, Melbourne-based designer Mimmo Cozzolino, co-founder of the All Australian Graffiti design team, published *Symbols of Australia*, a dense compendium of early Australian trademarks that designers still refer to fondly.[4] While similar material, in the US, continues to inspire a whole school of commercially viable and publicly admired pseudo-vernacular design, exponents of Australian vernacular such as Stephen Banham are the exception today. 'Some people, if you ask that question [about Australian design], will trot out a whole lot of old photographs of stuff that looks like signage out of Californian westerns – an English, colonial, Victorian thing,' says Graeme Smith. 'But I don't know whether I can see it now.'

Australian designers would sooner smash their G4s than resort to touristic clichés such as kangaroos, koalas and bush hats hung with bottle corks. Perhaps unfairly, the output of adman turned artist and entrepreneur Ken Done is often invoked as an example of a bogus form of Australiana. Done, subject of an admiring retrospective at Sydney's Powerhouse Museum in 1994, has a gallery and a shop in the city's harbour where he sells wall paintings and merchandise bedecked with his sun-drenched, good-life graphics.[5] 'It's second-hand Matisse rejigged with motifs of Australia, but it's not Australian,' insists Emery. Beechy suggests that it is Emery himself who has come closest to creating an Australian form of design. 'I believe he was one of the few to create a unique vernacular, a unique form of expression,' he says. 'Some would say it is relatively Dutch, but that's a superficial understanding of what he was trying to do. He was a severe modernist. He loves his Surrealism.'

Australia, as a landmass, is like nowhere on earth and nobody who has been to the outback can fail to be deeply impressed, and perhaps even changed, by the experience. As literary critic David J. Tacey shows in *Edge of the Sacred*, Australian literature has engaged obsessively and often fearfully with the country's vast, psychically threatening, unforgivingly harsh and largely uninhabited interior.[6] Only by experiencing a psychic connection with the landscape, suggests Tacey, will Australians learn to respect the 'mythic bond' between the land and its indigenous inhabitants.

So it is odd, looking at contemporary Australian graphic design, how little it seems to be informed by a strong sense of place. In my conversations with many Australian designers, few of them ever mentioned either the landscape or the Aboriginal people, who are so conspicuous by their absence from both the business and practice of design. 'I don't think we should necessarily go looking to be regional,' says Emery, an admirer of Tacey's work. 'But if we look inward, then we can discover what is true to the place and create a sense of place and a sense of meaning that is Australian. The visual manifestation of that will be unique.' For city-dwelling designers huddled on the continent's coastal perimeter, to embrace the land would be to 'look inward' in both senses.

Now more than ever, though, Australian design is swayed by the pressure of external forces. Giant branding consultancies see Australia as a small but attractive market with plenty of growth potential. These 'global players', with offices everywhere, bring with them a corporate vision that treats design as little more than a matter of local 'maintenance' of international brands. In 1988, Interbrand opened a Melbourne office. More recently, Landor affiliated with Sydney agency LKS; FHA Image Design, creators of the 2000 Olympics logo, sold 70 per cent of its business to FutureBrand; Enterprise IG acquired Horniak & Canny; Attik opened a Sydney office; and Garry Emery sold Emery Vincent Design's Melbourne office to Clemenger so he could start all over again. In 2004, Emery teamed up with British designer Vince Frost to form Emery Frost, with offices in Sydney and Melbourne. 'For me, design has got so confused with business that it's no longer design any more,' says Emery. 'It's basically marketing... I think it's the most boring thing in the world.'

Those on the consultancy side inevitably try to cast these developments in a positive light. They say it will lead to better training for designers, greater expectations of customer service among clients and higher standards of professionalism all round. According to one consultant, Andrew Lam-Po-Tang, writing on the AGDA website, another effect might be even faster adoption in Australia of overseas design trends (not that the process seems especially slow). 'Once the new ideas land in [an] Australian subsidiary via the internal network, personal networks will take care of disseminating the ideas into the rest of the design community.' What this would presumably mean in practice

**Poster showing logos
drawn from memory
by Australian
schoolchildren, 2000.
Design: Stephen Banham**

is more homogeneity, less regional difference and less chance of a specifically Australian approach to design finding national expression.

Perhaps it is no more than a coincidence, but the period during which most of the globals have arrived has seen the proliferation of an increasingly purified, uniform, neo-modernist design aesthetic. The change can be clearly seen in the output of a company such as Nova. A few years ago, their work was compositionally intricate, with overlapping letters, type-size changes, mixtures of serif and sans serif, and irregular picture shapes. Today, Nova use a severely simplified, impeccably tasteful sans serif palette familiar from the work of London designers such as Mark Farrow, North and Cartlidge Levene – all mentioned by Hastie. 'For us,' he says, 'it's a lifestyle thing, because we lead hectic lives and we thought: life doesn't have to be this hard, let's just simplify everything. So that's what we did and we've never looked back since then. Why come up with a hundred different looks in a portfolio? It almost dilutes your personality, anyway.'

Many of the most highly regarded practices – the ones people consistently recommend, when asked – employ this stripped-down style: Precinct, with offices in Sydney and Melbourne; Feeder in Sydney; 3 Deep Design and Fabio Ongarato Design in Melbourne. It is a forgone conclusion that almost any Australian cultural magazine – about film, fashion, architecture or design itself – will adhere to this inflexible dress code. Fabio Ongarato is perhaps the most exquisite and North-like of all in his pursuit of dynamically refined, Helvetica-based layouts that put maximum emphasis on sumptuously art directed photography, often for clients in the fashion industry.

'The whole Cranbrook/*Emigre* revolution – I went totally against that,' says Ongarato. 'It wasn't really my aesthetic. It wasn't clear enough. It didn't say things clearly or define things clearly. We started to do a lot of that clean, modernist style early on when the graphic environment out there wasn't like that at all. But it caught up very quickly.'

Mary Libro and Jonathan Petley of Feeder, coming into design from a slightly different direction – Libro from digital imaging, Petley from architecture – have reached similarly restrained conclusions. They enthuse about the tactile qualities of their minimalistic designs with unabashed delight, but this sensuality doesn't extend to their treatment of typography, which is set down on the page with deadpan, if not frosty, precision. 'We always think of the idea first and then we play around with that until we bring it down to its essence,' says Libro. 'The images are beautiful. The information is pertinent,' Petley observes of one of their pieces. 'You don't need anything more than that.'

While much of this neo-modernist work is undeniably accomplished and projects a seductively fashionable air (at least for the moment), there is nothing specifically Australian about it. The argument is sometimes made that Australia, lacking much of a history, is intrinsically a modern – and therefore a modernist – country. Wherever this aesthetic is applied, though, even in Europe where it originated, it now looks unimaginative and tired. Anything can potentially happen within the rectangle of the page or screen or billboard, so why default to such a predictable, aesthetically limited and culturally inexpressive range of possibilities? In discussion with Australian designers, it was surprising how many mentioned the old idea of the 'cultural cringe' – the anxiety that Australian culture might not match up to standards elsewhere. 'There is still a lot of cultural cringe,' says Penny Bowring. 'There are still a lot of Australians who don't have confidence in what we produce ourselves and will say that anything that's international has got to be better than anything that's local.' It is a moot point whether the Australian taste for neo-modernism is an example of this, or just a sign that in an age of globalization, everywhere is subject to much the same trends.

Other Australian designers pursue paths that seem richer in both local and critical possibilities. In Sydney, Advertising Designers Group has positioned itself as an ethical agency, producing carefully honed poster and ad campaigns that help to raise awareness, cut costs and benefit society, the consumer or the environment. In Melbourne, Studio Anybody started in the late 1990s with the intention of developing an alternative model of graphic-design practice. 'In focusing on concept-driven exhibitions, publications and installations, we hoped to develop alternative communication strategies, learn new skills, stay motivated and make people stop, laugh and reflect,' explains Lisa Grocott, one of the five partners. Grocott, a New Zealander, teaches postgraduate design at Royal Melbourne Institute of Technology (RMIT) and her academic way of approaching professional practice remains the exception among Australian designers, though it is shared by the other four members of the team. They have managed to combine self-initiated projects with work for the Australian clothing label Mooks, as well as the Melbourne Fashion Festival.

The central question for Studio Anybody is to what extent it will be possible to find more hard-nosed commercial clients who will permit an exploratory approach. The Dutch designers Armand Mevis and Linda van Deursen have visited RMIT and Grocott compares client cultures in the two countries. 'When you listen to people like Linda and Armand talk about the way that they can push clients, you want to believe that's possible here,' says Grocott. 'There's no reason for us to pretend that's just a Netherlands experience.' Even so, she confesses to doubts, describing a meeting with a potential client who described a job as a 'no brainer' and who seemed to feel she was making a potentially lucrative commission more complicated than it needed to be.

Talking to Australian designers, it is clear that design down under can no more be understood as a single kind of practice than it can anywhere else in the developed world. To compete at a high level for the biggest clients will require an increasingly focused approach, especially with the arrival in force of the global branding factories. 'We have to be serious about our businesses and we have to have something to offer, otherwise they're not going to take us seriously,' insists Ken Cato.

There is no way that the smaller or even medium-sized local design teams will ever be able to outdo the globals, so perhaps the answer, as elsewhere, lies in a different strategy – locating the overlooked gaps and occupying them. This is what the most far-sighted and promising designers are doing. The future of Australian design, as an exploratory cultural practice, will depend upon the success with which committed designers are able to prise open these spaces, negotiate relationships with sympathetic collaborators and offer alternative forms of culture that the big guns simply don't grasp.

STRUGGLING TO BE HEARD

Business is Booming,
poster announcing
demonstration, 2001.
Design: Inkahoots

In 2000, a small, not widely known design company in Brisbane called Inkahoots published a book celebrating its first ten years. The images were intriguing but what really struck me were the book's three texts. 'We work mainly in the community and cultural sectors,' wrote Inkahoots' directors, Robyn McDonald and Jason Grant. 'Not just because that's where the best work is, but because we figure our environment is already cluttered with sophisticated corporate imagery that often doesn't represent the community's best interests. Alternative visual messages struggle to be heard above the rowdy din of dominant media. They need to communicate incisively with compelling power and drama, or even quietly with careful subtlety, just to compete.'[1]

This was unusual. In the space of just 72 words, Inkahoots had used the word 'community' twice, evoking ideas about culture's purpose from the years before Reagan and Thatcher. By the 1990s, an ideologically defined conception of community had more or less disappeared from discussion of design. Young designers might encounter such ideas from older teachers, but they would not be perceived as central or receive any reinforcement from design's professional organizations and publications. Yet here was a fiery-sounding team of idealists in Queensland placing 'community' at the heart of its practice. What was it about Brisbane, I wondered, that encouraged this way of thinking and working? Might Inkahoots' approach be a paradigm for designers seeking to pursue socially concerned forms of practice?

As their book makes clear, Inkahoots' work divides into two phases. From 1990 to 1995 they operated as a public-access poster collective and since 1995 they have been a design company. Their guiding principles were shaped in adversity. In the 1970s and 1980s, under Joh Bjelke-Petersen, Queensland's pugnaciously authoritarian premier, civil liberties were constantly under attack. In 1977, his National Party–Liberal Party state government banned the right to march and more than 1,800 people were arrested for protesting about uranium mining in the state. Historian Ross Fitzgerald characterizes Bjelke-Petersen as a 'fundamentalist Christian, passionately anti-socialist and a fervent advocate of unfettered development'.[2] During his 21 years in office, cultural and intellectual life in the state was deeply demoralized.

In other parts of Australia, though, these were years of optimism and political growth. Many people were radicalized in the 1960s and early 1970s by protests against the Vietnam War; by the women's liberation movement; by the anti-nuclear movement; and by a growing interest in alternative lifestyles. Artists and others questioned art's role and there was a resolve, among community arts workers, to make art and art practice as widely accessible as possible. After the establishment of a national funding body, the Community Arts Board, community-based arts programmes proliferated. One of the more vigorous forms this commitment took was poster-making, which offered a cheap, simple and – in the form of silk-screening – readily available means of expressing dissenting points of view.[3]

In December 1989, Bjelke-Petersen's dark reign came to a long-awaited end. The idea to start Inkahoots arose the same year when Chris Stannard, Geoff Heller and Robyn McDonald – the only original member still with Inkahoots – teamed up, during a housing crisis in Brisbane, to work on a poster project for the Tenants' Union of Queensland. They set up shop, with funding from the Australia Council, in the concrete basement of the city's Transport Workers' Union building. They chose the name, Inkahoots, for its 'Australian-ness' and because they saw themselves as being 'in cahoots' with community activists; also because they worked with inks. The basement studio rapidly became a focus for radical groups and causes. Preparations for the Labour Day Parade, Lesbian and Gay Pride Week, and Reclaim the Night protests took place there, along with art workshops for people with disabilities.

Before going to university, McDonald had trained as a nurse. 'Because I had left school at 15 and gone straight into nursing, I felt I had missed out on an education,' she says. 'So I was going to uni in an old-fashioned sense to get educated or to learn about my society, my world.' She studied political science, art history and radical feminist philosophy, including the writings of Luce Irigaray and Julia Kristeva. Bob Weatherall, an Aboriginal elder and activist, was another significant influence on her political development. After gaining her BA at Sydney University, she took a diploma in illustration at Queensland College of Art. In 1987, inspired by Redback Graphix, she formed the Black Banana poster collective in Brisbane with two artist friends.

When I visited Brisbane in 2001, Inkahoots' old basement was empty, but the posters they pasted from floor to ceiling over a long rear wall had somehow survived, documenting their work for many causes: Child Care, Land Rights for Aboriginals, Australian Gay Games, International Women's Day, Men Against Sexual Assault, Reclaim the Night, Tenants' Union of Queensland, Rock 'n' Roll Circus and the West End Street Festival. A powerfully graphic poster by Stannard protesting about the Gulf War shows an American soldier against a black background, with the eloquently simple plea – 'don't do it!' In a vivid Warholian screen-print by McDonald, two couples – one gay, one lesbian – both naked from the waist up, embrace and kiss. Some un-known visitor to the basement had carefully defaced the poster with white paint.

Inkahoots was a late arrival among Australian screen-printing col-lectives. By the late 1980s, posters had a much diminished role com-pared to the 1970s, when political life, in the form of demonstrations and strikes, was more evident in the streets. Increasingly, high-impact professional advertising was colonizing this public space. Radical col-lectives were broadening their scope and diversifying. Community clients required a wider range of communication services and demand for commissioned work had increased. There was a need, too, for a more developed visual vocabulary to accompany political debate. In its idealistic attempt to serve the community, Inkahoots faced economic pressures familiar to other collectives. Members of the public using the studio often had no idea about the screen-printing process and educat-ing them was laborious and time consuming.

Although Inkahoots' early posters were pieces of graphic design, their makers were either artists, with a background in fine art, or they were entirely self-taught as visual communicators. The designs often have a raw, even 'amateur' quality and lack the finesse in handling typographic details that would be expected from professional graphic design. They relate to established conventions of community poster-making, rather than to any of the prevailing aesthetic design currents, whether traditional or experimental. McDonald doesn't recall the studio buying design magazines and books at this time, but the mastery of composition that she discovered in *The Graphic Language of Neville Brody* (1988) had a lasting impact when she saw it around 1990. 'I was a community poster-maker, I suppose,' she says. 'Seeing Neville Brody's work opened my eyes to the fact that we needed to open ourselves to influences.'

In 1994, Inkahoots advertised for another member. The job went to Jason Grant, who had briefly studied fine art at Brisbane College of Advanced Education before transferring to Queensland College of Art to do graphic design. Grant had an immediate impact on Inkahoots as a designer and a decisive effect on its development as a design consultan-cy. Stannard and other members departed and Inkahoots was formally wound up as a company, becoming a partnership between McDonald and Grant. Since May 1995, they have been based in a small, wooden studio, no wider than a garage, next door to the flyer-covered Grass Roots Resource Centre in West End.

Grant's personal philosophy was already highly developed when he joined Inkahoots at the age of 23. 'I started karate when I was about 14,' he explains. 'In traditional karate, the emphasis is on spiritual development and that really translates very clearly into ideas of social justice and democracy. But it comes from a non-materialist, spiritual dimension, which is very hard to explain. I started studying Zen and Eastern philosophy generally. It was a completely new world. I trained in Japan and my karate master was a Catholic priest. I had no interest in organized religion, but these things felt like deep realities to me.'

Grant read Marxist texts such as *Capital* and *The Communist Manifesto* and attended political rallies and street protests. 'I didn't see any reason to separate a personal agenda from a professional one. Right from day one at university there was the idea that design was there as a tool of capitalism. Although maybe I couldn't have articulated it at the time, that just didn't feel right. It felt like there should be alternatives.'

For Grant, too, Brody was a significant early influence. During his first year at Queensland College of Art, he read a manifesto-like text based on a lecture given in 1989 by Brody and cultural critic Stuart Ewen at the American Institute of Graphic Arts' 'Dangerous Ideas' conference. Ewen and Brody argue that in the contemporary world, 'Design no longer envisions, it advertises. Design no longer informs or educates, it blindly promotes the accumulation of wealth and power.'[4] Grant believed that it was essential to use contemporary graphic languages, since this was the only effective way even to begin to compete with highly resourced commercial forms of message-making.

Talking to Inkahoots' clients, it is obvious that it is not seen as a typical design company.[5] Clients know about the studio's background in community service and activism and, in some cases, they have worked with it for years. They believe that McDonald and Grant understand their activities and share a common cause. Karen Fletcher, a Brisbane solicitor and activist, recalls seeing Grant up against a line of police at the 'M1' anti-capitalist protest in May 2001. 'I thought: "Ah, this is why you've come up with this design idea, this is why you've given us this. This isn't about you servicing us. This is about you being part of what we are doing."'

Another client, Joe Hurley, a community worker at West End's Housing Resource Centre, sees Inkahoots' arrival in the area, after Grant joined the team, as a decisive moment. Hurley offers advice, information and counselling about tenant rights for people who are renting through government or community organizations, especially lower-income earners struggling to keep a hold in the inner city at a

No Vacancy, **poster for Inner Brisbane Housing Network, 2000. Design: Inkahoots**

OUT IT package - see

leaving town

B091

★

B076

SAVE $

B100

NO VACANCY NO SHELTER NO HAVEN NO HAR

HOUSE TRAINED

B110

NO VACANCY

welcome to Brisbane

EVICTING THE HOMELESS

The squeeze is on. There's no place left to stay in the Sunshine State! Is housing a fundamental human right or a luxury for the privileged? Can we get our governments to secure this right for ALL citizens?

time when Brisbane is experiencing a trend towards inner-city gentrification. He has worked with Inkahoots since the early 1990s and his office walls are covered with posters from earlier initiatives and campaigns.

In 2000, responding to public pressure about the visibility of homeless people in public places, the authorities began moving them on from parks, river banks, caves and thoroughfares – they were effectively 'evicted'. 'It was an outrageous attack on people who were so vulnerable,' says Grant. The Inner Brisbane Housing Network, to which Hurley belongs, resolved to protest and Hurley supplied Inkahoots with two pages of text for a poster. This was clearly too much information, so Grant edited and rewrote it – a role frequently undertaken by Inkahoots – placing the core message near the centre in a small but unmissable black box.

This is just one component in a multilayered communication that could, at first sight, appear random. It has a complexity that would once have been thought undesirable in a poster designed to communicate quickly and without ambiguity. The elements overlap and intersect to form a message both forthright in its declaration of what ought to happen – housing for all of Brisbane's citizens – and cuttingly ironic in its depiction of the actual state of affairs in the city. Queensland represents itself as the 'Sunshine State', extending a warm welcome to all visitors, but this generosity is withheld from some of its less fortunate citizens for whom there is 'no vacancy' in Brisbane. Those who live outdoors experience all kinds of weather conditions, sometimes with serious consequences for their health. Now there is a metaphorical sense in which the city authorities, too, are 'raining' on the homeless for reasons connected with financial gain and a political agenda that prioritizes the needs and sensibilities of the affluent. What makes the poster so engaging is the way it clothes these ideas in the most seductive and suggestive visual forms.

Since Grant's arrival, several other young designers have worked at Inkahoots. These designers, educated in the 1990s, were in some ways even more committed than Grant to new graphic approaches and styles. The studio has no stated hierarchy and all the workers earn the same salary, a situation that would be unthinkable in most studios in Australia and abroad. Inkahoots' partners take pride in not employing anyone in the formal role of art director to oversee the work, or attempting to fulfil that role themselves, though less direct forms of influence are probably inevitable. The problem has been to reconcile the studio's political principles with the younger designers' need for freedom of self-expression – a need that has been encouraged and shaped by the dominant values of a design culture that Grant and McDonald resist.

As Grant knows, the aesthetic 'revolution' in 1990s design was not driven by corresponding ideas of social and political change. Yet in reality, he writes, 'There is no such thing as an apolitical stance.... To ignore this is a VERY political stance.'[6] 'Radical' design's commitment to the endless 'new' fitted it perfectly for its cheerleading role in global consumer culture and, far from posing any challenge to the status quo, it was effortlessly assimilated by marketing and advertising. 'We bravely rip off style,' observes Grant, 'and we homogenise aesthetic diversity. We fuck promiscuously with typography and legibility but rarely with the dominant ideology.'[7]

The dilemma, for Inkahoots, is whether such styles can be reclaimed in a reverse manoeuvre that renders them once again authentically meaningful, this time within the sphere of socially concerned design. Or is this strategy inherently bound to fail? If bogus radicalism has become the very sign of the dominant ideology, how are these styles supposed to signify differently just because the context is switched? Or should they simply be regarded as a ready-made visual language familiar to everyone, which can just as easily be used for the delivery of alternative forms of message?

Another poster, created to announce the 'M1' blockade of the Brisbane Stock Exchange, as part of a nationwide series of protests, is based on a style of imagery often used for music and dance events. It shows a graphically simplified skull and crossbones, an 'anti-logo' drawn in outline like a pictogram, with a mushroom cloud erupting from the top of the skull. Below, in a stylized speech bubble, are the words 'BUSINESS IS BOOMING'. The degraded heading text, scanned from a shopping docket, refers to the electronic displays at the stock exchange. Nothing about the image would surprise anyone familiar with music flyers or CD covers, but its graphic vocabulary is a long way from the socialist realist, 'fist in the air' genre of protest.

'My view is that working people recognize good design when they see it and crappy design doesn't impress anybody,' says 'M1' organizer Karen Fletcher. 'Having something with design values has actually set us apart from a lot of the other propaganda that's around. People look at it twice. They don't look at it once and write it off. They're interested in what it's about.'

Visiting Brisbane, it is clear that Inkahoots' achievement owes much to the special nature of the city itself. Suburbs such as New Farm and West End feel like enclaves – slower-paced, anarchistic, refreshingly unobsessed with money. Brisbane is changing, though, and some of the qualities that seem so distinctive today may soon be eroded by economic forces. Inkahoots' pursuit of socially concerned design means that they earn considerably less than if they undertook projects for the commercial clients who sometimes knock at their door. The pressure to compromise can only increase.

Inkahoots' relationship with their community is organic. They care about Brisbane and draw their clients from a well-dispersed network of colleagues they have known for years. Without such deep roots, it is hard to see how a design company could flourish by undertaking this type of work, or how its personnel would acquire the motivation to serve in this way. Most young designers in the wealthy nations have not been exposed to the political passions and prolonged public struggles that are probably needed to inform a practice with Inkahoots' strength of engagement. Even for those who do have the commitment, there is little sense now of a national – still less an international – network of designers sharing similarly idealistic aims. 'We are fairly isolated,' admits Grant. 'The only time we have attempted to hook up with what we perceive to be individuals or groups within the movement, it hasn't really worked out, anyway, like with *Adbusters*. There doesn't seem to be any response from them.'

The question inevitably arises as to how long McDonald and Grant will be able to keep the studio going. Grant moved to London and worked there from 2002 to 2004 and McDonald, now in her forties with a family, has sometimes struggled with the restrictions of a lower wage than she could earn elsewhere. Inkahoots' strength of purpose in sustaining a socially concerned practice in the face of contemporary design culture's indifference is remarkable. For more than a decade, they have shown the continuing viability, in the right circumstances, of a form of engaged design that has few recent champions, though it remains, as they would argue, more vital than ever.

TASTE-FREE ZONE

If there is one quality in design that seems wildly overrated these days, it is good taste. Right now, with design in the ascendant as never before, it sometimes feels as though the entire developed world is gripped by a rampaging outbreak of impeccable taste, and wherever you go this taste seems to be much the same. No doubt habitual consumers of tasteful design, the sort of people who pore over Herbert Ypma's *Hip Hotels* and hang on to every directive from the likes of Terence Conran or Martha Stewart, assume they have discovered the access codes to a level of cultural refinement unavailable to lesser folk. For a short while, during the 1980s design boom, I remember feeling the same way. It was undeniably exciting dining out in Paris or Madrid in the latest sensation by Philippe Starck. At a certain point, though, I decided enough was enough. It is not that I refused such pleasures if they happened to come my way, but I certainly wouldn't make them central to my sense of myself.

In graphic design, there is nothing more limiting than flawless good taste. True, it communicates to those who happen to share its values. Too bad that its aesthetic repertoire is so restricted that it always communicates essentially the same thing. After all, what does it offer? Small type, almost invariably sans serif; nice, big photographs; plenty of exciting white space to admire – and that's about it. There was a time

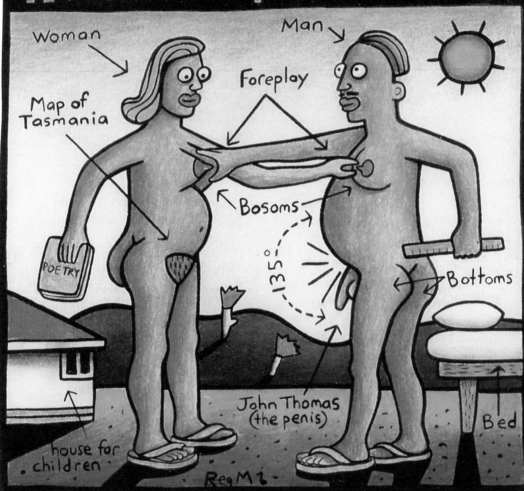

when this visual purity was a controversial, even radical statement, a bracing rejection of clutter and confusion. Plenty of designers still seem to believe that Swiss design in the 1950s and 1960s represented some kind of high-water mark. This typographic vernacular was already re-emerging in Europe in the early 1990s as a background to fragmentation and grunge. In reality, as anguished American complaints about 'zombie modernism' recognized, it had never gone away. After the blowout of deconstructive excess, many designers were happy to opt for a safe, familiar diet of Univers and Helvetica.

Don't get me wrong. I understand this style (frankly, there's not a lot to understand) and I admire some of its early exponents. I even think it has a place today in timetables and soporific art catalogue essays, though I would hate anything I have written to be presented in this way. As a reader, I can think of nothing more lifeless and off-putting than a page of Helvetica. It strips the prose of its voice, renders it dull and official-looking, and this was often the case even when the style was still fresh.

Call me a tasteless purveyor of civilization-endangering garbage, but I confess to deriving a great deal more pleasure and meaning from outright, taste-free vulgarity. On a couple of visits to Australia, I looked closely for the first time at the output of Mambo, the surfwear specialists. The company, founded in Sydney in 1984 by Dare Jennings – brother of Kate Jennings, the New-York-based novelist and poet – has 30 stores in Australia and around the world, though none in the US. Today, Mambo makes T-shirts, 'loud shirts' ('loud' is putting it mildly), surfboards, eyewear, caps, bags, wallets, watches, jewellery and ceramics. It is well established, but not, by global standards, a huge company.

Mambo's commitment to graphic expression is extraordinary by any estimation, and this vision comes from Jennings, who has an early background in printmaking and the music business. Under his loving direction, employing a cast of more than 15 regular contributing artists, Mambo has achieved a graphic identity that is rich, inventive, anarchic, protean and often genuinely funny. It ought to be a classic case study for branding's numberless practitioners, except that its unforced, organic development and its unfakeable authenticity as the expression of a unique company culture (not that Mambo would use such painfully leaden terms) could never be copied. If you consider Mambo's output as a 'text' – and words do play a central role in its world view – then, considered overall, it has the cultural complexity of a novel or film.

But our theme here is vulgarity. Mambo began life with a cartoon image of a flatulent dog and the bad odours just kept on coming. Its

Human Reproduction, image for Mambo T-shirts, posters and postcards, 1995. Illustration: Reg Mombassa

graphics are non-PC, often dubious, sometimes just this side of obscene. 'Mambo Etymology', a T-shirt, poster and postcard image by Reg Mombassa, probably Mambo's greatest and strangest artist, helpfully defines the meaning of crude sexual slang such as 'Crashing the yoghurt truck.' His 'Mambo Biology' image explains human reproduction in geographical terms ('The penis enters the map of Tasmania in the area of Port Arthur, proceeding rapidly up the Derwent past Hobart' etc.). Mambo has also, to some scandalized eyes, dabbled in blasphemy. Mombassa's Australian Jesus character is a three-eyed messiah shown, in one memorable image, distributing pies and beer to the crowd at a football match.

Vulgarity of content is matched by vulgarity of visual expression. According to Mambo's 'Declaration of Artistic Principles', 'Vulgarity finds its own context when helping to shift some big units'.[1] Mambo artists borrow from comic books, cartoon strips, vernacular typography and graphics of every variety, and the tackiest, most debased forms of illustration. No hang-tag or woven label is too small to carry a piece of intricately crafted Mambo art. Other companies also plunder these strands of popular culture, but Mambo does it with an energy, ironic conviction and gleefully irreverent good humour that has few equals anywhere. 'Calamity shall temper and harden our resolve as we destroy popular culture in order to save it,' declares a Mambo manifesto. 'We shall overcome hardships and exhibit a contemptuous disregard for fashionable truths, existing libel laws and contemporary standards of good taste.'[2] While the artists have careers in their own right, their work fits seamlessly into Mambo's pluralistic vision without diluting the qualities that made them distinctive in the first place.

There is no denying that Mambo embodies a very masculine kind of humour. Mambo's retort would be that surfing is still largely a masculine pursuit. The company's scatological conceits can be infantile, though the cleverness of the project as a whole arguably makes up for this. American rock-poster artist Frank Kozik's work has the same raw intensity, but Mambo's vulgarity lacks his psychotic edge. Some Mambo artists might share Kozik's obsession with 'man's ruin' (women and booze), but you won't find fluffy rabbits shooting up or bears eating children pictured on Mambo products. In truth, Mambo is the very model of a responsible company. Australian Jesus – 'Not afraid to do a woman's work,' according to one T-shirt – has feminist leanings. The whole point of 'Mambo Theology' is to attack religious intolerance. Mambo supports groups such as Greenpeace, the AIDS Trust of Australia and a Sydney support centre for victims of drug and alcohol abuse, and makes forthright statements about Australian politics on its website.

Mambo's jubilant embrace of vulgarity is actually a commitment to content. The multiplicity of graphic signals allows the company to say so much more. During my visit to Mambo's Sydney headquarters, Dare Jennings told me about an exhibition he had seen in Tokyo of some ultra-fashionable British designers' work. He thought it was empty: a few abstract gestures, some blurred photographs of nothing in particular. Of course, much as they savour it, Mambo's use of vulgarity is knowing and deliberate and, for this reason, one might argue that it represents a concealed form of good taste. Above all, though, it is a pointed reminder of how bloodless and unadventurous, how reluctant to take real risks with content, so much graphic communication has become.

DESIGNING PORNOTOPIA

In an issue of *Maxim* magazine published in 2001, the editors hit on a novel way of presenting a series of woman-pleasing sexual positions to their male readers. They photographed a pair of miniature crash-test dummies going through their paces in a variety of domestic settings. The six-page story was visually explicit in a way that would not have been possible in glossy news-stand titles even ten years earlier. Cheeky tableaux demonstrating the 'sumo straddle', the 'harvey wall-bang-her' and 'crouching tiger, hidden penis' left little to the imagination, and nor, for that matter, did the text. Even so, the faceless, metal-jointed, anatomically neutered male and female dummies were carefully judged not to offend against prevailing standards of good taste, if that is the right word to use. The conceit was unexpected and even funny.

In more ways than *Maxim* probably intended, we are all crash-test dummies now. It is not just that we are having sex – nothing new there – but that we are obsessed with its display in our media as never before. No previous society has possessed the technological means or the social and moral willingness to broadcast and explore its sexual desires on this scale and to this extent. We are taking part in a huge social experiment. Sexual images envelop us. They crash into us. They mould our reality and perhaps they mould us. We can only speculate about how they will ultimately change our relations with each other and

Image from Suzi Godson, *The Sex Book*, Cassell Illustrated, 2002. Illustration: Peter Stemmler

transform our society, for good or ill, but change will certainly come. As the *Maxim* feature showed, with its breezy consumer tips for complete satisfaction, these images are already reshaping expectations of the kind of sex we should experience.

Behind the eruption of sexual images into global visual culture lies pornography. In the last decade, the rapid normalization of porn and the complete turnaround in social attitudes to it is one of the most momentous developments in everyday life. For a reminder of the case against pornography, most forcefully expressed by the feminists, turn to the late Andrea Dworkin's lacerating 1981 book *Pornography: Men Possessing Women*. 'We will know that we are free when the pornography no longer exists,' she writes. 'As long as it does exist, we must understand that we are the women in it: used by the same power, subject to the same valuation, as the vile whores who beg for more.'[1] In a moving afterword, she describes the mental cost of three years spent studying porn: 'Pornography has infected me. Once I was a child and I dreamed of freedom. Now I am an adult and I see what my dreams have come to: pornography.'[2]

In the early 1980s, the video revolution began the change in attitudes by delivering moving-image hardcore pornography into the home. With the arrival of the Internet – the moment when many people who would never have ventured into a sleazy sex shop in search of a videotape saw pornography for the first time – it was permanently on tap, even in the workplace. More recently, in the ever-popular *Friends*, a TV series loved by pre-teens, jokey references to pornographic imagery and scenes built around watching it became quite routine. If a porn habit was once viewed as evidence of brutishness or inadequacy, qualities a person might want to hide, it is now a subject for some of the most admired fictional characters on TV to brag about. Being at ease with porn, as a fact of life, is all part of being a cool, funny, attractive individual.

Mainstream media cannot equal porn's explicitness, although it edges closer all the time, but knowing that audiences are familiar with these images allows publishing, advertising and now design to go much further than they would once have dared. The media has a symbiotic relationship with porn. In the last decade, there have been countless articles in magazines and papers about the industry. By covering porn, the media borrows some of its dirty glamour and sense of danger, while in return it confers legitimacy, making porn a topic of interest and discussion like any other. In 2001, Martin Amis, something of a specialist in the depiction of seedy underworlds, filed a report in *Talk* magazine on the $10 billion porn business. Whatever Amis's intention – he seemed to want the women he met to escape from the porn life – the story's effect, as presented on the page, was stylish and celebratory. 'To millions of American men these women are movie stars,' cooed the title. *Talk*'s creative consultant, former Benetton creative director Oliviero Toscani, shot group portraits of five naked, high-heel-clad porn stars – Chelsea, Adriana, Chloe, Lola and Temptress – fitting snugly into each other's ample curves.

As you might expect, it is in magazines aimed at young people that the fascination with sexual imagery derived from pornography has been at its most intense. The technique is often to tease the reader while implying that, if only the editors were allowed, they would be happy to show us everything. In 2001, the fashion and style magazine *Sleazenation* put a couple who appeared to be having sex in the back of a vehicle on its front cover. In the opening spread of a story called 'Hardcore!' about changes to Britain's obscenity laws, published in a special issue of *The Face* devoted to everyone's favourite subject, cloud-like blocks built from the letter 'x' mask the unprintable parts of a scene involving a woman and two men lifted from a sex magazine. A few pages later, *The Face* assigned three spreads to clumsy, pixel-style graphics constructed from little pink rectangles by photographer Sølve Sundsbø, better known to style-magazine readers for his glacially perfect digital fashion pictures. It did not require much ingenuity to discern what the stylized body parts were up to – in the unlikely event that the tasteful headline 'Come over my tits!' left any room for doubt. Their purpose was less obvious. The images were not aesthetically engaging after the initial impact and it is hard to believe anyone found them arousing. Perhaps they were a kind of graffiti, pulling down their pants to an authority that would not let them go the whole way and show these activities as high-res pictures.

For a decade now, men's magazines have felt free to plaster their pages with images of scantily clad women that would once have pro-voked cries of 'sexist!' and their readers have lapped it up, while gleeful-ly tucking into the pornography to which these titles continually refer. It was only to be expected that these cultural influences would begin to surface in graphic design, though this is a more recent phenomenon. The four-man German design team Eboy epitomizes the digital designer take on sex. On the back cover of their book *Eboy Hello* (2002) they show a line drawing of a naked woman with an Eboy tattoo on her arm. She stares suggestively at the viewer, her hand cups an invisible shape, and her long tongue appears to be licking something unseen.

Drawings of naked women are scattered throughout the book. One spread shows two reclining women with their lips parted, one with a discarded beer can on her torso; in each case their genitals are displayed. Another presents photos of the four Eboys posing in their workspaces opposite yet another drawing of an attractive naked woman.

The book's brief text attempts to head off any possible criticism. Eboy's references, we learn, 'come from trashy sci-fi, action movies, Top Trumps cards or porn.... what saves their fascination with boys' toys from the jaws of juvenilia is the rich seam of humour and irony that runs through it all. Cheesy pin-ups are pushed just that bit further to become satirical rather than titillating.... "Our pictures are never driven by moral ideas or a moral view of the world," they say.'[3] Two questions spring to mind. First, is it really possible to be satirical without having any moral ideas? Satire implies some sense that the world falls short in certain ways and could be improved, and this is a moral view. So, taking Eboy at their word, as people with no moral ideas to offer in their visual creations, it is not at all clear in what way their images of women could be construed as 'satirical'. If, despite this, we still prefer to give them the benefit of the doubt, then a second question arises: where exactly does the so-called irony in these images lie and what are they satirizing? Women who pose for the kind of 'cheesy pin-ups' to which Eboy's images allude? Men who like to look at them? Or the designers themselves, who chose to fill their book with these babes?

There is no satire. Eboy, like other designers who flirt with sexual imagery, display these linear pin-ups as trophies in their gallery. The designers are clothed and the images of them that intersperse the book project a sense of ownership. The naked, tattoo-sporting women are portrayed as simpering, compliant, Eboy-branded playthings, just as they are presented as playthings in men's consumer magazines. Feminism would once have had no trouble locating the sexism in these images, but in 'post-feminist' times, when the concept is applied so rarely in everyday speech, the situation is murkier. The tendency now is to stop at the surface, to enjoy the vector illustrations for their fashionable style, to find the sexiness cool and avoid going any deeper than that. Any 'irony' amounts to nothing more complicated than a shared understanding, in which women are expected to collude, that such depictions are unobjectionable good fun.

Interestingly, Peter Stemmler, an Eboy member based in New York, was chosen as illustrator of *The Sex Book* (2002), a contemporary guide to sexual matters that is unusually forthright, even by the standards of the genre. Here, within a more clearly defined context, one might almost detect a trace of satire in the images, although this cannot be what the publishers had in mind. While the colours are hot and lurid, yet again suggesting the pervasive ambience and visual temperature of porn, the spidery, inexpressive outlines of faces and bodies convey little sensuality or warmth. In an illustration for a discussion of sex and the older guy, a man gropes a young woman's breasts less like a tender lover than an obnoxious cradle-snatcher, while in a section on children and sex a weird kid clutches a copy of a girlie magazine called 'Ficken' to his chest. It doesn't look too healthy, but clearly not everyone agrees.

The mixed-up messages in these illustrations reflect the confusion that surrounds the whole issue of sexual images. Militant feminist campaigners against pornography tended to overstate their case, arguing that all pornography encouraged violence against women and lobbying for its prohibition on these grounds. In Robin Morgan's famous phrase, 'pornography is the theory, rape is the practice'. Other feminists argued just as persuasively against any kind of censorship. To impose restrictions, they felt, was to imply that a sexual norm really existed and to sanction 'the policing of desire'. As Linda Williams writes in *Hard Core* (1990), her ground-breaking analysis of pornographic film: 'Given the many possible viewpoints on sexuality, we need to beware of arguments that state that pornography is inadequate to the whole truth of sexuality. Here the implication is that a whole truth of sexuality actually exists, outside of language, discourse, and power. This idea, I argue, is the central fallacy of all the anti-porn feminist positions: that a single, whole sexuality exists opposed to the supposed deviations and abnormalities of somebody else's fragmentation.'[4]

In the years since this was written, the 'fragmentation' of sexual possibilities has become a source of enormous fascination in contemporary culture. Forms of sexual behaviour that would once have been vilified as signs of a degenerate character now raise barely an eyebrow. Sadomasochistic imagery has become commonplace in music videos, advertising and fashion. Porn stars appear as cultural icons on TV chat shows. Documentary-makers visit Manhattan dungeons and whorehouses in the Nevada desert to interview the women and their far from embarrassed clients. These may be questionable gains, but unarguably positive developments have come from the process of liberalization, too. Gay people have achieved increasing levels of social acceptance, and thanks to feminist campaigners women's right to explore their sexuality is widely recognized now. For better or worse, women have joined men in the sexual marketplace as consumers of sex products and women-orientated porn.

So all the signs suggest that the future will bring many more sexual images. Since pornography is the primary source of this imagery in our culture, it is hard to imagine what non-pornographic public representations of sexuality would even look like. The pornographic imperative is now so ubiquitous in language and imagery that it can hardly fail to influence the way in which young people think about their bodies, their desires, and what they expect from their sex partners. A print ad for Hooch clothing, showing young men and women on cellphones, is designed to look like a series of prostitute cards. The copy lines read: 'Make me filthy, I'll always come clean.' 'Feel my stiff one!' 'Get your hands on my XXXL.' This is supposed to be a laugh, but the tone is juvenile and the cumulative effect of ads such as this is a decrease in subtlety, a coarsening of feeling, and a denial of the right to make intimate personal discoveries at your own pace, rather than at a speed determined by commerce.

This, finally, is what makes sexual imagery so problematic. These days we prefer not to think about the possible downside of porn. How does early exposure to it, particularly as a child, affect development? What does it mean to be an emotionally mature individual and is the regular use of pornography consistent with that? These images seem to be an invitation to an endless pornotopia of pleasure, but what might we be losing along the way? Without reliable answers, we simply do not know what we are doing to ourselves.

Until recently, sexuality was understood to be a private matter and for most people, most of the time, despite our voyeuristic urges, it still is. It was even thought to have something do with love. But intrusive, omnipresent sexual imagery erodes the private/public distinction and evaporates any sense of mystery. In 2004, a campaign for Trojan condoms appeared on London's streets. The two posters showed close-ups of the faces of a man and a woman in orgasm. The advertisers probably saw this as a breakthrough, though it was not the first time the idea had been used. The only shocking thing, in contemplating these supposedly ecstatic images, was the realization that, within such a short space of time, all this writhing and moaning in public had become such a turn-off.

COLLAPSING BULKHEADS

J.G. Ballard's *Crash* is one of the most original and disturbing British novels of the past few decades and for many of his admirers it is his most extraordinary book. When it was published in 1973, Ballard was already recognized as a writer of great visionary power. *Crash* went even further than his earlier book, *The Atrocity Exhibition*, in which some of its sexual and technological themes first emerged. It is a novel that tests the limits of the reader's taste and sympathies in the most profound ways and it has always provoked strong reactions – positive and negative.

The publisher's reader, a psychiatrist's wife who was given the task of assessing Ballard's manuscript, famously declared: 'The author of this book is beyond psychiatric help.' According to British novelist Will Self, the editor who worked on *Crash* would lock it in his desk at nights to prevent colleagues from being appalled by its pages. Self has said, 'I only have to look at a few paragraphs of *Crash* to feel I am in the presence of an extreme mind, a mind at the limits of dark imagination.'[1] This was a commendation. 'How many people are there who'd want to read a book like *Crash*?' Ballard once asked. 'Not many.'[2]

Yet *Crash*, described by Ballard himself as a 'psychopathic hymn', did find a following. It became a cult book, appealing to the kind of reader who also liked William Burroughs, a writer Ballard has constantly praised. It was the type of novel a post-punk rock band might enthuse about in the music press. Over the years it has appeared in French, German, Italian, Dutch, Spanish, Portuguese, Greek, Finnish and Japanese translations. After several false starts with other would-be directors, *Crash* was filmed by David Cronenberg in 1996. In Britain, the film's release prompted a moral panic. Set in the motorways, access roads, flyovers and multistorey car parks around London Airport (now Heathrow), the book imagines a society in which the car crash has become the focus of a deviant new sexuality. At the centre of the story, narrated by a director of TV commercials called Ballard, is 'hoodlum scientist' Dr Robert Vaughan, who drives around photographing crash victims and having sex in cars. Vaughan dreams of dying in an accident with film star Elizabeth Taylor.

During his research, Ballard acquired *Crash Injuries* by Jacob Kulowski (1960), an American medical textbook full of comparisons of wounds caused by different makes of car. Ballard's language fuses clinically precise descriptions of sex acts and terrible injuries with an almost hypnotic lyricism: 'In his vision of a car-crash with the actress, Vaughan was obsessed by many wounds and impacts – by the dying chromium and collapsing bulkheads of their two cars meeting head-on in complex collisions endlessly repeated in slow-motion films, by the identical wounds inflicted on their bodies, by the image of the windshield glass frosting around her face as she broke its tinted surface like a death-born Aphrodite, by the compound fractures of their thighs impacted against their handbrake mountings ...'[3]

I read the hardback first edition of *Crash* as a teenager, soon after it came out. I was already a devotee of Ballard's other books, but I loved *Crash*'s extremity, its sense of moral danger, its willingness to probe dark areas of the psyche, and the toxic beauty of its prose. When the paperback appeared in 1975, I read the book again. In 1980, on a trip to Paris, I saw the Livre de Poche translation and bought it – it contained an introduction by Ballard not then available in English. Over the years I collected editions of the book, partly to see whether any publisher would ever produce a visual interpretation that achieved the concentrated power of the quotation above. Ballard is an intensely visual writer. He has said that he felt more at home with artists such as his friend Eduardo Paolozzi and Richard Hamilton than he did with other writers. He attended 'This is Tomorrow', organized in 1956 by Hamilton and others at the Whitechapel Art Gallery, made collages, staged an exhibition of crashed cars in 1969 at the New Arts Labs in London, and often referred to Surrealist painters such as De Chirico,

Crash by J.G. Ballard, Panther Books, 1975. Illustration: Chris Foss

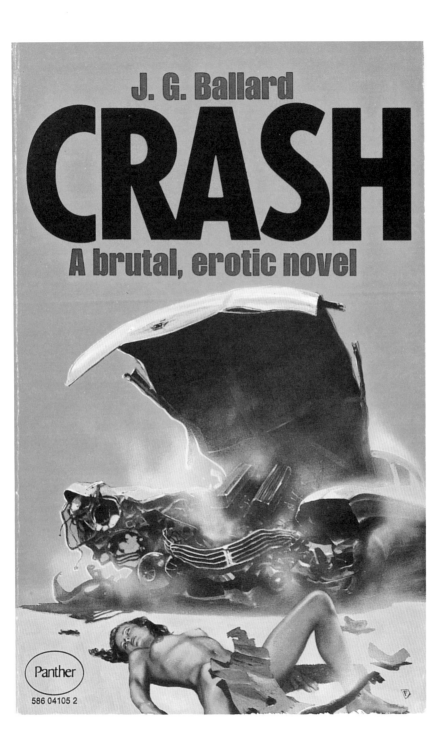

J. G. Ballard
CRASH
A brutal, erotic novel

Panther

586 04105 2

Ernst and Dali. In 'The Coming of the Unconscious', an essay written in 1966 for *New Worlds* magazine, he described the images of Surrealism as 'the iconography of inner space'.[4]

This is rich and provocative source material for designers and illustrators. How to visualize a piece of writing which is prepared to be, in Ballard's words, 'openly pornographic' as a literary stratagem? On the whole, though, image-makers have been defeated by *Crash*. A book that ought to have inspired covers to match and reflect its status as an underground classic has often received visual treatments marked by incomprehension and evasion. I was curious to know how Ballard viewed this, as a writer with such a strong sense of the visual. He didn't wish to be interviewed – reviewing the covers would, he suggested, be 'rather too close to an autopsy on myself' – but he was willing to make notes on some of them if I sent him photocopies.

The first jacket, published by Jonathan Cape in 1973, shows a jutting gearstick, presumably intended to be phallic, in front of a towering three-dimensional title that occupies most of the cover. This still rankles with Ballard, who describes it as 'monstrously bad, one of the worst book jackets ever – for sheer ugliness and crudity, impossible to beat'. Few of the Ballard hardback covers produced by Cape in the 1970s and early 1980s were any good. The first UK paperback edition of *Crash*, however, illustrated by science fiction artist Chris Foss, retains its power. 'Superb, in many ways the best ever,' notes Ballard. 'Quasi-realistic, but in the right way, like a movie poster of the 1950s – brought into brilliant focus by that line – "A brutal, erotic novel".' Foss, an illustrator of *The Joy of Sex* (1972), treats the image as an opportunity for lurid, pulp-style exploitation. There is nothing quite like this scene in the book. The ruined car smoulders with menace, its twisted bonnet rising above the woman's naked body like a predator's gaping maw.

This cover established the principal iconographic elements – woman and car – that feature in many interpretations of *Crash*. In 1985, the novel was reissued as part of a new, oppressively black-bordered series, with an illustration by James Marsh showing a red-lipped Amazon at the wheel, clad in studded leather. This connected the book with emerging trends in fetish clothing and a fashionable flirtation with S&M, but it had nothing to do with Ballard's vision. By 1993, the woman was reduced to a pair of pouting red lips framed by a shattered rear-view mirror – it resembled the kind of airbrush illustration in vogue 20 years earlier. Ballard dismisses the cover as 'too lipsticky – too "neat"'. His 1974 introduction, which might have offered additional clues for visual interpretation, is reprinted in both editions. *Crash*, he writes, is 'an extreme metaphor for an extreme situation, a kit of desperate measures only for use in an extreme crisis.... Will modern technology provide us with hitherto undreamed-of means for tapping our psychopathologies?'[5] Neither cover shows any hint of these concerns. The tacky Livre de Poche edition, in which a car's radiator grille metamorphoses into a flesh-licking tongue, once again turns the vehicle itself into the protagonist and misses the point.

Where interpretations of *Crash* by male image-makers tend to present female sexual personae in the most obvious and unrevealing ways, as victim or vamp, missing the unbridled perversity of the book's female characters, women designers and image-makers have been inclined to neutralize the book's violent eroticism. A 1985 US paperback designed by Carin Goldberg, with wide-spaced 'new wave' typography, arbitrarily transplants *Crash* to the American desert, where a faceless female who looks like a misplaced fashion model wanders away from some totemic car parts scattered in the dust. The cover's Surrealism-lite bears only the most tenuous connection to the novel. Photographer Clare Godfrey's cover image for the 1995 UK edition treats *Crash* as a kind of ecstatic fairground ride. The hot neon colours and chaotic superimpositions relate to a scene in which Vaughan and the narrator cruise the motorways while under the influence of LSD, but the image is strangely depopulated and *Crash*'s relentless sexual content is suppressed.

Crash is peculiarly resistant to attempts to summarize it with a single image. Its synthetic literary method depends on the conjunction within a verbal image of phenomena that are usually discrete. Ballard insistently establishes geometrical relationships between the body parts and postures of his characters and the technology that surrounds them: 'By entering her vagina among the metal cabinets and white cables of the x-ray department I would somehow conjure back her husband from the dead, from the conjunction of her left armpit and the chromium camera stand, from the marriage of our genitalia and the elegantly tooled lens shroud.'[6] In the late 1980s, collage and montage became increasingly prevalent means of expressing thematic complexity on book covers. If ever a novel called out for a mode of evocation based on fragments and juxtaposition, it was *Crash*, but it was 1994 before an American design team explored this possibility.

Michael Ian Kaye and Melissa Hayden's cover for Noonday Press makes *Crash* look like the cult novel that it is. 'I loved the book,' says Kaye. 'It was so much about cars and sex that it seemed stupid to hide that. We went to a junkyard. We were both really into this project.'

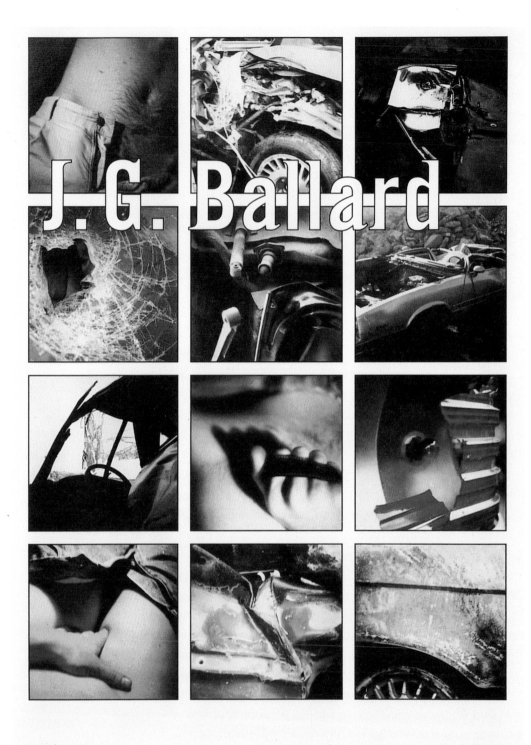

J. G. Ballard

Crash

Hayden's boyfriend was also involved in the shoot and, for once, both sexes are presented as equally implicated in Ballard's nightmare marriage of technology and desire. It was Hayden's photographic concept, but at the junkyard they passed around a Polaroid. The grid of 12 pictures on the cover shows smashed and crumpled bodywork, a hand clutching a roll of film, a man's jeans open at the fly with the suggestion of an erection and a woman's hand delving for her crotch. A glimpse of breasts or buttocks can be seen through a broken windshield. 'They all represent little blips of the experience,' says Kaye. 'Using the grid speaks a little more to the futuristic quality without being so literal. It was about lots of little ideas making up the whole.' The 'garage font' title typeface, a sans serif to which serifs have been applied selectively, adds to the mood of unease. With cult-like understatement, Kaye positions the title in the bottom right-hand corner as a kind of full point to the design.

Ballard had never seen this version of *Crash* until I sent it to him. Publishers do not always provide authors with copies of foreign editions. He found the cinematic treatment 'a bit too literal – if the novel is a psychotic hymn, this hardly suggests it'. But then no cover has succeeded in fully expressing the delirium of *Crash*. The 1996 UK film-tie-in version, which Ballard, a supporter of Cronenberg's interpretation, does admire, was another missed opportunity. The cover is based on a scene showing actress Holly Hunter (Helen Remington) straddling James Spader (James Ballard) in the front seat of a car. While the image conveys nothing of the perversity of either book or film and only hints at the role of the car, it does carry an erotic charge, acknowledging sexual interaction as the book's subject in a way that few *Crash* covers have dared.

The cautious handling of *Crash*, even now, is all the more surprising when one considers the prevalence of pornographic imagery in contemporary culture. As a work of bizarre prophecy, the book was far enough ahead of its time to be truly shocking, though only a fool would imagine that Ballard thought we should crash our cars for sexual thrills. The phenomenon and meaning of the collision has become the subject of cultural criticism in essay collections such as *Car Crash Culture* (2001) and *Crash Cultures* (2003), and the spectre of Ballard's narrative invariably haunts their pages. *Crash*'s explosive collisions of flesh and metal are, as Ballard says, a metaphor, taking social tendencies and following their trajectories to discover where they might lead. In his introduction, he notes that 'we live in an almost infantile world where any demand, any possibility, whether for life-styles, travel, sexual roles and

Crash by J.G. Ballard, Noonday Press, 1994. Design: Michael Ian Kaye and Melissa Hayden

identities, can be satisfied instantly'.[7] If that was true when the book was written in 1973, it is even more the case today. At the time, Ballard described the book as 'cautionary' and 'a warning', but he has wavered on the question of whether *Crash* is a moral indictment. In 1997, he told cultural critic Mark Dery that the novel illustrates the process by which 'formerly aberrant or psychopathic behavior is annexed into the area of the acceptable' and he pointed out how the proliferation of new communications technologies was aiding this process.[8]

In December 2003, GQ ran a story about 'dogging', a sexual subculture in which people use the Internet to arrange meetings where they have sex in parked cars while others watch. The item was illustrated by the Hunter and Spader shot used on the cover of *Crash*.

THE SEX DETECTIVES

Not long ago, I saw a man in the Institute of Contemporary Arts book shop in London impulse-buying a book on the strength of no more than its title and cover design. The pink, padded volume was sealed in a cellophane wrapper, like all the other copies, and the man didn't ask the sales assistant whether he could unwrap it, though he did ask whether the book was any good. The assistant declined to offer an opinion one way or the other, but the man bought it regardless. The book was called *Porn?*

Did it deliver the goods? That will probably depend on how closely he paid attention to that question mark and, more pointedly, to the typography of the single word on the cover set in one of Louis John Pouchée's decorative alphabets. Using a pre-Victorian display type ornamented with Edenic bunches of fruit to signal the twenty-first century's favourite growth industry is a wonderfully sardonic touch.

Porn?, conceived by Tom Hingston Studio and *Dazed & Confused* magazine, offers a plethora of porn-related projects by photographers and a few artists.[1] Try as it might, the book confirms just how hard it is to say anything new about the subject, especially if our starting point, both emotionally and literally, is that we have seen it all before. While art might once have been the medium by which many encountered sexually provocative material, it has been left in the dust by the Internet's power to pump 24-hour 'transgression' into our homes. That is probably why some of these image-makers prefer to arrive on the scene, like clue-seeking detectives, after events have transpired. Anuschka Blommers and Niels Schumm show used condoms littering patches of bare ground; Larry Sultan pictures the empty sets and locations, the furniture and mattresses, where porn gets made.

If these images suggest something deeply forlorn in our hyper-sexualized culture, others revel in more ambiguous forms of distaste. Sølve Sundsbø digitally grafts women's heads on to the bodies of men grasping their cocks and splatters the images with hideous typographic cum-ons. In one of the most telling projects, fashion stylist Simon Foxton and designer Stephen Male construct a series of convincingly real fake porn mag covers complete with cover lines – *Prostitute Weekly*, *Meat Pie*, *Cucumbers and Beauty* ('This issue: birth defects special'). Yes, there is something for everyone out there in 'Pornoland', as Mark Irving dubs it in his languidly non-judgemental introductory essay. Is it just me, or would risking a little judgement – pro or anti – be a more interesting and productive position to take at this point? The more avidly we peer at porn and the more we claim, if only by implication, to enjoy this peering, the less we seem to want to consider what it might be doing to us. By transcribing advertising copy – 'Transexual sluts', '1-800 teen clit' – on to drawings of anxious men, Paul Davis hints at the psychic cost of porn's routine, dehumanizing callousness.

There is very little actual sex in *Porn?*. Perhaps it seemed too obvious. On the other hand, in the current climate, showing active genitalia and asking whether such an image must necessarily be porn is a truly provocative question. What is it that makes porn 'porn'? Is it the mere fact of showing explicit sex? Is it a certain attitude on the part of the makers, the seller, the buyer? If it is the buying itself that makes something porn, then the *Porn* book is porn. Is it a question of how you use the image? If it makes you come, then it is porn. Or is it, more subtly, a question of codes of representation, the way the images are conceived and shot? Porn often shows ugly things, but it also shows them in an ugly way (some might like that, of course) with harsh, unmodulated lighting and negligible compositional skills. The images purport to be representations of 'pleasure', but in their brutal mechanics, they convey little understanding of what pleasure means.

In *Porn?*, Sean Ellis applies the kind of photographic values to fucking that you would normally see in an ad. In some ways, his pictures observe the conventions of the glossier kind of porn. The woman wears stockings and shoes and the man is reduced to a hard-on. They look more like ads for sex than sex itself, but they have a beauty and a conviction that is startling in this visually degraded context. In form if not outlook, they suggest the possibility of a sexual image-making that escapes the generic constraints and stigma of porn. Or is this to overstate the significance of style?

BARING IT ALL

Until quite recently, it was often said that design should be anonymous. Not knowing who had created a design was thought to be a virtue, a sign that the design was doing its job. Design was functional and practical; its role was to convey a message, or to give you something to sit on. Humble items such as the paper clip, which seemed to have existed for ever, were praised as quintessential examples of design. Of course, there were always a few designers who became famous. Some, like Raymond Loewy, actively courted fame and became familiar public figures, with their faces on magazine covers. Others became internationally famous within the design profession. But most people working in design paid lip service to the idea of anonymity, most were anonymous themselves and for tens of thousands of designers this continues to be the case.

In the last 20 years, though, design has changed. A class of design stars has emerged and for anyone going into design now it must be clear that fame is an achievable goal. There are various reasons why this has happened. In broader terms, it corresponds to deep changes within the culture. Warhol's prediction that in the future everyone would be famous for 15 minutes has come to pass. In the new celebrity culture, you can be famous for being famous, with no real achievements to your name. Docusoaps and game shows take ordinary members of the

Artist's Opinion, page from *Whereishere*, 1998. Design: Stefan Sagmeister. Illustration: Kevin Murphy

WhyDoTheyFuckEachOther?IsTherePenetration?JustForSho
Artist...MarleneMcCartyWasRecently'Out...ed'By
...ericaFor...WorkingAsADesigner(SheRunsBu...requin
...rk).Micha...elSchirner,AGermanAdvertisingGuy...HasAPre
...vincingA...rgumentThatInTheTrueTraditionOf...eonardo,
...iliAndMich...elangelo,AdvertisingReallyisArt(AndFin
...WeKnowitT...odayisSomethingDifferentAlt...ogether).H
...ThatArtHi...toricallyWasAlwaysProduce...dToGlorify
...hty,-InMich...elangelo'sTimeTheChurchA...ndTheEmper
...e20ThCentur...yTheChurchAndEmperorH...aveLostTheir
...TheMightyGuy...AreTheCorporationsA...ndTheyAre
...AdvertisingA...gencies.MakesP...fectSense.IT
...hesisToSever...Curat...orsAnd...tists.EverySi
...OfThemThough...itWa...Bullsh...tButNotOneCan
...hAGoodCounterA...gume...t...YearsAgoTheMus
...ModernArtMounte...A...igh/LowShowinte
...BrokeDownTheBar...iersBetweenHigh
t)AndLow(Advertis...ing/Design).InitWork
...LowlyTomatoSoupCa...sAndTransformedT
...oHighTomatoSoupCan...s.SomeOtherPeopleTo
...ichelinGuyAndModes...omethingHigherOuto
...thSuchASillyPremise...mActuallySurprised
...edALotOfTheArt.Dam...enHirstSaysInHisNewB
...tHeisActuallyMoreInf...uencedByAdvertising/
...ThanByOtherFineArt.?...heBookMostCertainlyS
...BeATrueCollaboration...BetweenHimAndDesign
...hanBarnbrook.Someho...wArtAndDesignHaveMo
...erTogetherInEngland...AndMaybeJapan)Thanin
...tes.TomatoisDoingALot...OfNonClientExperimente
...ThatSomeWouldCall'Fi...eArt'.SeenInTheContex
...igniThinkTheyAreRathe...InterestingAndProba
...dMakeAGoodInterrupt...onWhenInsertedIntoAB
...egularTvAdvertising.As...FineArtTheySuck.InThe
...tOfAMuseumiFindTheW...orkOfBillViola,MonaH
...TonyOurslerMuchMore...Interesting.SoHere's
...hink:OneDifferenceBe...weenArtAndDesign
...ThCenturyisThatDes...ignStartsWithAComn
...AndArtStartsWithin...TheArtist.ThatWoul
...hatPublicArt,-AP...rt...cularSizeSculpture
...rticularSpaceToF...xpre...sAParticularPro
...otArt,ButDesign...WhatSee...msToSetArtApart
...esignisThatArtOf...enLeaves...tsMeaningOpen,
...interpretedInM...anyDifferent...ways,itsUpToThe
...oSeeItInHis/He...OwnWayAndAl...ThatShit.iAlways
...tedThatAGoodN...umberOfArtists...AreTooLazyOrTo
...oMakeUpTheir...MindsAndLeaveEv...erythingSwim
...mbiguityAsAR...esult(MuchLikeSom...eOfThatBullsh
...edDesignFro...mTheLast10Years-Ca...sonAtAl.-That
...ntMakeUpit...sMindAboutitsMeaning)....TraditionalD
...nTheOther...andHasToTransportAMe...aning,Conten
...essageInA...WayThatPeople(OrAtLeast...argetAudi
...nderstand....BrianEnoStatesThatArtMigh...NotBeThe
...Object...selfButThe'ArtExperience'You...HaveWhen
...counterT...heObject.ThatWhatMakesAWork...fArt'Good
...Someth...ngThatAlreadyisInsideTheObjectBu...Someth
...Happe...nsInsideYou,TriggeredByTheObject.T...hisDefin
...mplifi...esMattersGreatlyBecauseitAutomatic...allyinc
...sign...AtLeastGreatOne)intoArt.itDoesNotMat...erWh
...illit...ButitDoesHaveToMoveYouOrTouchYouB...eAny
...Art...AndDesignWouldStopFuckingEachOtherTh...eyReally
...ReallyGoodSexInstead.ChancesAreTheirKidsWouldBeGre

public and turn them into national figures. Tabloid newspapers spin endless stories about the activities of this new celebrity class. In such a climate, the idea that designers – a group with no lack of ego – would dedicate themselves to lives of unassuming anonymity is absurd. Moreover, design's support and promotional system is much more developed now. Countries such as Britain, the US, Germany and Japan have always published stylish design magazines. These days, from Mexico to Russia, from China to the Czech Republic, many countries have their own specialist publications, which glorify the works of the same roving band of transnational design stars. Lecture invitations, conference appearances and exhibitions add to this group's growing prestige. Ten years ago, only the most stellar and durable design figures would find themselves lauded in career monographs, which design-book publishers regarded as commercially risky ventures. Today, publishers compete with each other to sign deals and publish lavish, celebratory tomes. None of this would be happening if there were not a huge appetite within the design profession, particularly among younger designers, to admire, learn about and learn from its inspirational figures. At the same time, there is a growing interest outside the design world in the people who shape our visual reality. Three-dimensional designers are the usual beneficiaries of this attention, but occasionally a graphic designer – Neville Brody, Tibor Kalman, David Carson, Bruce Mau – achieves wider renown.

Stefan Sagmeister belongs to this new international class of famous designers. He wears the acclaim lightly, but he seeks it nonetheless. On the title page of his monograph, *Sagmeister: Made You Look*, there is an inscription in his own handwriting that reads 'Another self-indulgent design monograph'.[1] This is engaging and disarming, but if he really felt the book was unacceptably self-indulgent, why would he publish it? Clearly, he doesn't actually think this. The inscription continues, in parenthesis, underneath: '(Practically everything we have ever designed including the bad stuff).' Most designers wouldn't dream of including their bad stuff, so again it is hugely winning. What it shows is that Sagmeister is so confident that the good stuff is good that he can afford to show the bad stuff as a sign of his honesty. In his New York studio, Sagmeister has created some excellent design and this is the single most compelling reason why his work is worthy of attention. His fame, though, is something of a paradox. Sagmeister's work is remarkable, in the context of the 1990s, not because it represents a startlingly new departure, but because it represents the persuasive reassertion of ways of designing that had been rejected by many of his colleagues. It is no coincidence that interest in Sagmeister's work grew in the mid-1990s as these other, supposedly more radical design approaches lost their lustre.

My own introduction to Sagmeister came around this time, when he sent me three of his early CD designs. They all made a powerful impact, though my reaction to each one was quite different. I was immediately attracted to *Telling Stories to the Sea* (1995), a collection of Afro-Portuguese music. Its cover is delicately eccentric, with a wobbly, handwritten title that runs down into the transparent spine. The booklet typography has a playful, improvised informality that matches the music perfectly. A hole punched through the cover becomes an ear piercing, a fish eye, a bullet hole in a target, and so on. I have played it many times since it arrived out of the blue. The second album, H.P. Zinker's *Mountains of Madness* (1994), struck me as one of the most effective pieces of CD packaging I had ever seen, and many others have felt the same way. Sagmeister, too, rates the cherry-tinted jewel box as one of his finest pieces of work. The plastic case acts as a red filter, and when you pull out the booklet the man's benign features turn to rage. In the same way, you can X-ray the group members and see their insides. I put the CD to one side as a piece of design worth keeping, but I didn't bother to play it, suspecting it would disappoint, and when I finally did, years later, it proved to be mediocre hard rock. It was a triumph of packaging over content. The third CD, *The Truth Hurts* (1995) by the thrash-metal band Pro-Pain, has a truly disturbing cover. It shows a photograph of a dead young woman, taken in a morgue. The Y-shaped cut in her torso, made during the autopsy, has been sewn up with jagged stitches. I had seen the photograph before, but its use on a pop record, along with police photos of murder scenes, seemed unforgivably insensitive. I didn't know what to do with it. I certainly didn't want it. I couldn't think of anyone who would want it. I didn't feel inclined to send it back to Sagmeister, so I threw it away. Later, Sagmeister said he wanted to produce design that 'touches the heart'. In their different ways, each of these CD designs had certainly succeeded in doing that. They were all unforgettable.

FROM BREGENZ TO MANHATTAN

Stefan Sagmeister was born on 6 August 1962 in Bregenz, Austria. His parents, Karl and Karolina Sagmeister, owned a fashion-retailing business and his two elder brothers went to business school before becoming fashion retailers themselves. Sagmeister reacted against this and, in 1976, began studies at the local engineering school. He was not suited to this line of work and at the end of the third year he transferred to a college in Dornbirn, where he gained his first experience of graphic design working on a small left-wing quarterly called *Alphorn*, providing spot illustrations and learning to set type with IBM electric typewriters. In 1981, after graduating from Dornbirn, Sagmeister moved from Bregenz to Vienna. He applied to the Hochschule für Angewandte Kunst, sat its demanding three-day examination, failed to get in and spent a year improving his drawing at a private art school. In 1982, on his second attempt, he was successful. Sagmeister's professor and supervisor, under the 'masterclass' system operated at Angewandte, was Paul Schwarz, a disciple of Parisian poster artist A.M. Cassandre, and Sagmeister found the emphasis on Art Deco rather limiting.

More useful, in the long run, was an introduction to Hans Gratzer, director of the Schauspielhaus, who agreed to consider using designs proposed by Sagmeister and some fellow students for the theatre's next production. Gratzer chose Sagmeister's proposal and this led to a long-term relationship between the theatre and the students, who called themselves Gruppe Gut. The young designers worked competitively and Grazter would choose the idea he preferred. Often it was Sagmeister's. His posters tended to be strong, simple designs, with a single image dominating the space and lines of type filling the width at top and bottom. In 1985, a play called *Abendrot* (Evening Red) was written in a matter of days to protest against a plan to construct a power station in Hainburg. Sagmeister's poster shows the type printed on a crumpled Austrian flag so the words become distorted, with entire letters missing, though the sense is clear. In 1984, when Gratzer launched a campaign to save Vienna's 100-year-old Ronacher music hall, he asked Sagmeister to design the posters. Here, too, Sagmeister's later inventiveness began to reveal itself. One of the posters incorporates perforated theatre tickets and another shows the Ronacher and other Viennese theatres laid out as star signs in the night sky. 'Suchen' (search), says the copy line. In all, Sagmeister produced 35 different poster designs. The Ronacher escaped demolition.

In 1986, Sagmeister graduated from Angewandte with a first-class honours degree. In *Sagmeister: Made You Look* Peter Hall points out that his thesis project, 20 interactive postcards, laid the groundwork for many of his later projects, showing his emerging predilection for tricks and inventions. One postcard, for instance, folded out into a sundial that could be adjusted to the local time zone. During his final year, Sagmeister applied for a Fulbright scholarship and, largely as a result of his projects for the Schauspielhaus, he was successful. In autumn 1986, he began his studies at the Pratt Institute in Brooklyn. Two projects in particular stand out from this first interlude in New York. Asked to produce a business card for his girlfriend that cost no more than a dollar a card, Sagmeister used an actual dollar bill. The name and contact details were printed on the note, which was folded in a particular way to assume the size and thickness of a business card. On another occasion, Sagmeister was going to be visited by a shy friend, who feared that New York's women would not want to talk to him. Sagmeister printed posters with his friend's photograph and the plea 'Dear Girls! Please be nice to Reini', and pasted them up on New York's Lower East Side. Reini arrived to find he was already a talking point, and a conversation with a woman about the poster led to a relationship. 'I always call this my one successful ad campaign,' says Sagmeister.[2]

After three years in New York, Sagmeister returned to Vienna to do community or military service. As a conscientious objector, he was assigned a job in a refugee centre outside Vienna. The few projects that he shows from this period suggest he was marking time and that he had yet to find either his direction or an outlet for his talents. In 1991, on a trip to Hong Kong, he decided to explore the city's design scene and wound up being offered a job as a typographer at the Leo Burnett advertising agency. Shortly after he took up the post, the agency suggested that he start the Leo Burnett Hong Kong Design Group. Most of the work consisted of routine brochures and promotions for hotels, airlines and department stores, but projects aimed at the creative community provided more scope for playful invention. Sagmeister was frustrated by the conservative quality of most Hong Kong design in the early 1990s and the sheer 'niceness' of it all. His opportunity to create a stir came with a commission to design a call for entries for the annual competition of the Advertising Agency Association Accredited (AAAA). On the completed poster, four Chinese stand in the harbour with their hands cupping their mouths, calling for entries. Below them, the same scene is shown again, only this time the men have turned their backs to the viewer and are bending over, baring their behinds. Much of the poster's impact comes from Sagmeister's decision to illustrate the scene in a traditional Cantonese trade-painting style. The poster achieved its aim. It stimulated a 25 per cent increase in competition entries, but it also scandalized many people. A rival agency, Dentsu, refused to attend the award ceremony and tried, without success, to organize a boycott of the competition. In retrospect, 'The 4A's' is clearly the moment when a distinctively 'Sagmeister' approach to design emerges with confidence. Daring and perhaps even tasteless subject matter is lightened and made acceptable by a pleasingly sharp visual wit.

In spring 1993, Sagmeister moved back to New York to take up a position running the studio at Tibor Kalman's design firm, M&Co. Kalman had built an unrivalled reputation as a wisecracking, opinionated, self-styled 'bad boy' of American design. A self-taught designer, he opposed the design profession's slickness and its self-serving values and conventions. Sagmeister, recognizing that M&Co could be the ideal home for his talents, had called the studio many times during his spell as a Fulbright scholar, hoping for a job. Now, finally, he had one, but it was not to last. Kalman announced that he was closing down M&Co, and after just six months Sagmeister was on his own. In October 1993, deciding to stay in Manhattan, he launched his own studio, Sagmeister Inc.

WRITTEN ON THE DESIGNER'S BODY

It has been extremely common in the last 10 or 15 years for young designers to start their own studios and collectives soon after graduating. There is great pressure on those who want rapid success to evolve a distinctive style while still students. By comparison, 20 or so years ago young designers usually worked for established design companies for a number of years, learning all aspects of the craft and business, before setting up their own companies (if they did this at all). Sagmeister's route towards autonomy has followed this traditional path. Given the impact he has made in recent years, in his thirties, his development might seem surprisingly unhurried. It also seems to have proceeded according to no obvious plan. The ambivalent quality of Sagmeister's ambitions can be gauged from a 1984 entry in his diary: 'I'm convinced that I'd like to be a famous designer, on the other hand this desire is so silly. (And will generate a lot of stress). This is bullshit. I mean all that matters is to try to be good, try to be honest.'[3]

As a New York designer, Sagmeister has presented and promoted himself with great confidence and a highly idiosyncratic personal style. Many designers have exploited photogenic good looks in their publicity photos, but few have put a high degree of emphasis on their personal appearance to create an image, still less to build a 'myth'. One who did was Tibor Kalman. The cover of Kalman's monograph, *Tibor Kalman: Perverse Optimist* (1998), features a painting of Kalman by a Bombay studio, which has been used so often it has become a kind of logo. (Sagmeister has said that the monograph is his favourite design book.) In another well-known image, Kalman poses with a pencil clenched crazily between his teeth. Sagmeister's skinny suits, slightly long hair and floppy fringe give him the look of a rock star. He enjoys being photographed, and for his 30th birthday he made a party invitation featuring a different image of himself for every year of his life. On the card announcing the opening of his studio, Sagmeister showed two photos of himself wearing nothing but his socks. Two strips of removable masking tape, one significantly longer than the other, covered his private parts. Having removed them, the viewer could decide which image of his manhood had been digitally manipulated. In 1998, invited to contribute a project to the book *Whereishere*, Sagmeister submitted a spread consisting of the words 'where is here' scratched into his freckled back, and a full-page, larger-than-life-size image of his testicles.

The idea of self-mutilation was taken a stage further in a poster created the following year to announce a Sagmeister lecture for the American Institute of Graphic Arts (AIGA) at Cranbrook Academy of Art, near Detroit. Sagmeister asked an assistant to carve every word of the text into his torso and on to his arm, using a scalpel. It took eight hours to complete the task and by the end Sagmeister was experiencing considerable doubt and pain. He subsequently revealed that the inspiration was a photograph of the artist Catherine Opie with a children's drawing cut into the skin of her back. Many artists have used their bodies as canvas and subject matter, and some, like the Vienna Actionists, have mounted violent assaults on the self.[4] Considered from this standpoint, Sagmeister's actions may seem less remarkable. However, within the context of design, as a piece of *typography*, literally inscribed in blood, the poster is without precedent. This image, which has been widely reproduced, would in itself have been sufficient to make Sagmeister's name and it has had a lasting impact. At a time when so much design portrayed a simulated and artificial reality, Sagmeister delivered an electrifyingly real image, full of narrative implications, and grounded in an aspect of life with which every viewer could empathize – our all-too-vulnerable flesh.

Sagmeister is inclined to make light of his use of his body in this way. He says that being naked is 'no big deal for me' and points out that nude and topless public bathing are central to Viennese life. He also acknowledges that taking one's clothes off for the camera 'seems to get everybody's attention here in the States every time', so he is clearly capitalizing on his exhibitionist side as a sure-fire way of attracting attention. He knows that if it has worked once, it will probably work again. The British designer Vaughan Oliver has also appeared naked in photo-

graphs used in his own designs, but again the impact comes from the context, since this is not, as a rule, something that designers do. One could also see it as an aspect of Sagmeister's drive to be open and honest. He exposes himself for inspection, as if to say to the viewer: this is all there is. (Or turns it into a joke by suggesting that there might be more to him than you assumed, as with the naked portraits that announced the opening of his studio.)

In *Made You Look* – the title is revealing in itself – he exposes himself in other ways. He includes work that he regards as bad. He grades each of his projects from 1 (highest) to 5, and grants only two of them, the Reini poster and the H.P. Zinker CD, his highest rating. Even more unusually, Sagmeister reveals how many hours his studio worked on a project and what they received in payment. The 220 hours that went into H.P. Zinker netted the grand sum of $1,800. Throughout the book, he includes extracts from his diaries, which he has kept since the age of 14. (He regards the decision to keep a diary, along with the decision to keep his studio small, as the two best business ideas he has ever had.) Presenting the diary entries in his own handwriting, as though he is inscribing his notes directly on to the book's finished pages, works in a number of ways. It adds an extra layer of textural interest, it introduces a note of anti-formalist discordance, but most crucially it brings us closer – at least, it appears to bring us closer – to the designer himself. 'If I want to touch somebody's heart with a piece of design,' says Sagmeister, 'it has to come from my heart, it has to be true and sincere…. The audience of my design piece will feel if I'm honest, if it comes from my heart.'[5]

ALWAYS REMEMBER: STYLE = FART

Sagmeister summarized his approach to design in a simple phrase that he wrote on the wall of his Manhattan studio: 'Style = Fart'. The wording was a typically Sagmeister touch. It was direct, it was provocative, its meaning could not be plainer and it had a scatalogical flourish (even now this is not a word widely used in polite company). For a while, it became his miniature manifesto. When Sagmeister threw a party to celebrate his studio's fifth anniversary, he printed it on a whoopee cushion. In 1997, he designed a poster for the AIGA's biennial conference in New Orleans. Just above the conference title, 'Jambalaya', he inserted a handwritten line, saying 'And always remember', and underneath he showed a photo of his studio wall, declaring 'Style = Fart'. Thousands of American designers saw the promotional poster, and Sagmeister had prepared a second message for this

Sagmeister Inc. on a Binge, **exhibition poster, 2003. Design: Stefan Sagmeister. Photographs: Tom Schierlitz**

captive audience. The poster also featured a brief passage taken from an essay by Robin Kinross in a book about the Dutch designer Karel Martens: 'The danger of idea-based design is that it produces simplistic one-concept pieces, which, once you have got the point, become merely irritating. One finds this, the banality of the 'one-liner', in much American and British work of the 1950s and after.'[6] This was more ambiguous. Did Sagmeister agree with this assessment of 'idea-based' design, or was he challenging it? In graphic design debates, style and idea are often seen to be at variance, as though a designer must pick one or the other as the medium for communication. If Sagmeister rejected style, then presumably he was against the quotation and for ideas. Or did he perhaps think that idea-based design's methods were fundamentally sound, but that the ideas needed to be more compelling?

Certainly, Sagmeister is working within the tradition of idea-based design. A key early influence on his thinking was Bob Gill's book *Forget All the Rules about Graphic Design. Including the Ones in this Book.* Gill, an American, was an important figure in the development of this approach. He moved to London in 1960 and became a partner, along with Alan Fletcher and Colin Forbes, of Fletcher/Forbes/Gill. Gill and his colleagues aspired to produce designs that were surprising and original graphic solutions to communication problems. This required the designer to let go of any preconceptions about how design is supposed to look and, clearly, if a designer has a strong personal style, then he is starting with the assumption that a design should look like one of his own designs. 'If I could express the uniqueness of what the problem was trying to communicate with an image which was valid *only* for that problem, then I would have invented a unique image,' writes Gill.[7] The *idea* was so important that Gill argued it ought to be possible for a designer to describe it to a client over the phone; the client should be able to understand it and become excited by it without even seeing it. He conceded, though, that the idea still had to be visualized in a way that did it justice. 'The design decisions must not look arbitrary. They should look inevitable.'[8] Gill liked to claim that it was impossible to tell the difference between his early designs and those he had produced 30 years later.

In Britain and the US, this was the dominant approach to graphic design in the 1960s and 1970s. By the 1980s, many designers educated to believe that this was the correct way to design had started to challenge this assumption. In London, Neville Brody was hugely influential in popularizing an approach based on a strong and instantly identifiable personal style. Older designers tended to reject this kind of work as 'style graphics', refusing to see that stylistic choices and details could be the embodiment of an 'idea', and that a lot of this new work made subtle play with codes of communication that its intended audience understood perfectly, even if its critics did not. By the end of the 1980s, as designers began to explore the huge potential of the Apple Macintosh, idea-based design's simplistic 'one-liners' looked increasingly dated, patronizing and irrelevant to many young designers. They had a huge appetite for visual complexity and they preferred to focus their attention on typographic experiments and new approaches to type design. Some of the rationales for this new way of designing were theoretical, most notably at Cranbrook Academy of Art, where students read post-structuralist texts by Barthes and Derrida and began to wonder how deconstructionist ideas could be applied to design. It did not take long before they, too, were accused of peddling a fashionable new style. By the mid-1990s, when Sagmeister opened his studio, 'deconstructed' design – however challenging it might have been at the outset – really had degenerated into a clichéd global style. Far from signifying deep thought, it often seemed to signify only thought-free self-indulgence.

Sagmeister's work in the 1980s for the most part simply ignores these challenges to the orthodoxy of idea-based design. If his work now seems highly contemporary in a way that his early output does not, it is because he has found a way to hold true to his belief that it is the idea that counts most, while responding to aspects of contemporary design. His brief exposure to Kalman must surely have been influential here. In the 1980s, Kalman's M&Co reinvigorated the New York tradition of idea-based design with work that was smart, witty, knowing, stylish and hip. Young designers who worked at M&Co, such as Alexander Isley and Stephen Doyle, played a vital role in developing this approach and, when they left M&Co, they took it with them. Kalman was a tireless agitator for design with worthwhile content and his decision to shut down his studio, to concentrate on editing *Colors* magazine, was a gesture of total commitment. Sagmeister shares the view expressed by design educator Katherine McCoy that content is all: 'The most rarefied design solution can never surpass the quality of its content.'[9] By the time Sagmeister Inc. opened its doors, an updated idea-based design was thriving in New York and Sagmeister's contribution has given added weight to this persistent tradition.

The studio's typography for the *Telling Stories to the Sea* CD booklet gave an early indication of Sagmeister's ability to reconcile established approaches with the new typographic mood. Each spread relates to a different artist and receives its own treatment. In one layout, the type rains down like Apollinaire's calligramme 'Il pleut'; in another, the rough-hewn letters resemble graffiti on a whitewashed wall. The type was repeatedly photocopied to increase the sense of skewed imperfection. In a 1996 poster for the AIGA's 'Fresh Dialogue' series of lectures, featuring a talk by Sagmeister, he presents a couple of cows' tongues, which poke out, with phallic abandon, from inky, hand-drawn letters. Sagmeister's use of his own handwriting for all the text recalls many a 1970s album cover, but it also relates to the scrawled informality of so much 1990s 'grunge' typography. His most extraordinary fusion of established ways of problem-solving and the new aesthetic came the following year with the 'Jambalaya' poster. In the 1980s, Cranbrook Academy of Art designers such as Jeffery Keedy and Edward Fella experimented with an approach they called 'anti-mastery' as an antidote to the smooth perfectionism of so much professional design. Fella created dozens of posters in which he systematically disregarded and inverted every textbook rule of 'correct' design. 'Jambalaya' is a product of a design climate in which these assaults on design convention have been absorbed, taken to heart and even normalized. The fact that a national design organization could publish such a communication to promote its most important event indicates the degree to which American design had come to embrace an anti-aesthetic that would once have seemed to threaten its very existence.

The poster is meant to be funny and it is funny, but as so often with Sagmeister there is a slightly disturbing edge to the humour. When he was six, he saw Dr Heinrich Hoffmann's book *Struwwelpeter*, which has unnerved many a child. In one poem, the 'red-legg'd scissor-man' bursts into a room and cuts off little Konrad's thumbs because he persisted in sucking them. In the early 1990s, for a Viennese company called Frank's Disaster Art, Sagmeister designed a business card showing a running aardvark sliced in two. He suggests that memories of Konrad lay behind his decision to decorate the front of the 'Jambalaya' poster with two running, decapitated chickens, an image unlikely to have endeared him to any vegetarians among the AIGA's membership (and was he suggesting that designers run around like headless chickens?). Sagmeister asked participants in the conference to provide quick self-portraits on round-cornered stickers. Most complied and these are simply stuck on the image, while the various design credits take the form of a handwritten Post-it note. The information side of the poster is a masterpiece of haphazard construction and slapdash detailing, a riot of scrawled headlines, crooked paste-up, last-minute additions, humorous asides, and ornate doodles that look like the work of someone with too much time on his hands. Almost every centimetre of off-white space is filled with something, except for a small area that Sagmeister labels 'White space dedicated with love to Massimo Vignelli' – a staunch upholder of modernist principles who might have been expected to loathe the poster.

In 1996, the rock star Lou Reed asked Sagmeister to design his latest CD, *Set the Twilight Reeling*. As with his earlier music projects, Sagmeister filled the booklet with a series of typographic interpretations of the songs. On the promotional poster, handwritten lyrics follow the contours of Reed's face like a series of tattoos expressing his deepest thoughts. For the cover of Reed's collected lyrics, *Pass Thru Fire* (2000), Sagmeister used irregular, hand-rendered characters, embossed so they feel like scar tissue when you touch them. This is just a foretaste of a 470-page book that is genuinely transgressive by the conservative standards of literary publishing. Sagmeister gives each of Reed's albums a different typographic treatment intended to reflect its emotional character. For the Velvet Underground's *Loaded*, he spatters the verses with drips that blur the letters they touch. Selected lines from *Street Hassle* turn through 90 degrees, cutting across the other lyrics. The words of *Magic and Loss* fall away and entire songs quake with inner tremors. In *Set the Twilight Reeling*, a ponderous black bar gradually retreats up the page and disappears. It showed a high degree of commitment to the interpretative possibilities of design – and considerable faith in Sagmeister – for Reed to allow his body of writing to be treated in such a cavalier fashion. Despite *Pass Thru Fire*'s stylistic similarities to projects such as Avital Ronell's *The Telephone Book* (1989) or the *Strange Attractors: Signs of Chaos* catalogue (1989) designed by M&Co for the New Museum of Contemporary Art in New York, Sagmeister's aim is not deconstruction in an intellectual sense, but to use design as a compelling medium for the expression of feeling. His gestural devices are often distracting, but what they demonstrate, once again, is his willingness to appropriate, for his own purposes, typographic approaches regarded ten years ago as the province of the avant-garde, and to apply them to products aimed at the popular mainstream.

HOW TO TOUCH SOMEONE'S HEART

In recent years, Sagmeister has shown signs of frustration with the possibilities of design. In their work, graphic designers come into contact with many other kinds of cultural producer – artists, film-makers, musicians, writers and architects. They take a close interest in these art forms, as viewers, readers and listeners, often insisting that they derive more stimulation from these fields than they do from design. Designers cannot fail to be struck, too, by the degree of attention and prestige accorded to other cultural activities. Few designers win such acclaim. Above all, designers envy the power that art forms such as music and film can exert on their audiences. In a lecture titled 'Is it possible to touch somebody's heart with design?', Sagmeister expressed this concern: 'I've seen movies that moved me, read books that changed my outlook on life and listened to numerous pieces of music that influenced my mood. Somehow, I never seem to be touched quite the same way by graphic design. I know the comparison is not all that fair, after all, movies do have 90 minutes to do all that heart touching, books have several days, while most graphic design has to connect in seconds.'[10]

What Sagmeister wants is to produce work that has a lasting impact on those who see it. As an example of a piece of design that affected him in this way, he cites the sleeve of King Crimson's album, *In the Court of the Crimson King* (1969). Barry Godber's cover painting shows a man's face in nightmarish close-up. He appears to be terrified. One can see up his nostrils and deep into his mouth, and the lack of type only intensifies the 12-inch sleeve's power. Sagmeister is not alone in reacting to the image so strongly – I vividly recall the first time I saw it as a schoolboy – and maybe he underestimates the extent to which audiences are affected by certain kinds of design. One only has to look at old packaging for even the most banal domestic products to be reminded how deeply graphic signals can touch us. In cases where the design's content has more complex meaning and resonance in the first place – as with record covers, book jackets or film posters – these signals can be even more affecting. Sagmeister's decision to concentrate on music packaging when he opened his studio seems to acknowledge this. It may be that immersion in design as a practitioner reduces its mystery when one tries to be an ordinary viewer again, whereas, for the audience, it retains its disruptive power to come out of nowhere and take the emotions by surprise.

Some of Sagmeister's frustration stems from the struggle all designers face to find clients who will allow them to work at their best. In clients such as Lou Reed and David Byrne, Sagmeister has collaborators with an exceptional degree of imagination. In a diary entry, he notes how Reed told him that, no matter what level of success you reach, 'the bullshit just never stops'. In other words, there are always awkward people and situations to negotiate to ensure that good work gets done. Sagmeister has considered learning how to work in another medium, such as music or film, but concludes, in another diary entry, that, 'Instead of giving up on graphic design, I should try to reinvent it for myself.'[11] At the same time, he expresses concern that so much talent is poured into small-scale projects which few people see, while at the national and global level design is frequently banal. 'We should be designing soda bottles, postal trucks and huge commercial Web sites instead of leaving those jobs (which really do have cultural impact) to the marketing/branding idiots.'[12]

Yet it is hard to see how a mass-market item such as a fizzy-drink bottle could ever achieve the wayward presence with which Sagmeister endowed Skeleton Key's *Fantastic Spikes Through Balloon* (1997), when he drilled a grid of 81 holes through every page of the CD booklet. Or why an ordinary item would need such eccentric design. A bottle of soda might refresh you and the brand managers might try to spin an elaborate brand message about what makes their drink so different, but in the end it is just a drink. It cannot have the range of meanings carried by a collection of songs or a film. The Skeleton Key design was a quirky yet carefully targeted departure from the norm that would only be seen and fully appreciated by fans of the band. What does it matter if this audience was small, so long as the design made a real connection? Isn't there a fundamental contradiction between the idea of connecting with someone in an intimate, personal way (touching a like-minded individual's heart) and trying to find the common denominator that will elicit an identical response from a mass audience (touching everyone's heart)? Why fall in with a political way of thinking that takes it for granted, for largely commercial reasons, that bigger must necessarily be better?

A YEAR OF LIVING DANGEROUSLY

In October 2000, Sagmeister took a highly unusual step. After seven years of running his studio, he had decided to shut down his office and not accept any client work for a full year. 'On the surface, the year before had been the most successful to date,' he explained, 'our designs had won gold medals from Warsaw to New York, from London to Moscow and the then-booming economy filled our coffers. Underneath it I had less and less fun in the office, the work was getting mediocre and repetitive.'[13] Sagmeister wanted space to experiment and time 'to dream up bigger pictures'. He planned to re-evaluate what the studio was doing and decide what it was he wanted to say through his work. It was an audacious move and he prepared for it by announcing his intention well in advance. If everybody knew about the plan, then he would not be able to back out.

Sagmeister's year off was further evidence of his need to create design that counts. His work is distinguished by its grip on reality. He aspires to clarity and rejects the obfuscatory language and underlying, exclusionary purpose of 'art speak' and 'corporate speak'. He can make startling images, but much of his design's impact comes from its carefully considered qualities as an object, as a thing you can touch. Now that so much design looks like the product of a computer (because it is), his approach seems all the more satisfyingly physical and tactile. In a brochure for New York fashion designer Anni Kuan, his girlfriend, Sagmeister cut letter forms from strips of cloth and laid them out as words on the studio floor. For the Move Our Money campaign, which aimed to persuade the US government to redirect money from military expenditure to social causes, he devised a small card not much bigger than a book of matches. By sliding its central panel, challenging facts appeared in little windows: for the $17 billion it takes to build 10,000 nuclear weapons, the US could hire 425,000 new teachers. David Byrne's book *Your Action World* (1998) may have been postmodern in theme and hard to pin down in outlook, but Sagmeister embodied it in tangible yellow plastic. When you lifted it out of its transparent plastic carrier, half of the letters on the cover stayed behind because they were stuck on the bag itself.

Showing the same practical ingenuity in his personal arrangements, Sagmeister has solved many of the dilemmas that can lead a designer away from the projects he would prefer to be doing. He lives and works in the same studio, which he was able to buy outright so he has no mortgage to pay. He has continued to work with just a single designer and a trainee, so he doesn't have the pressure of burdensome overheads. All of this meant that he was free to undertake his year without clients. (His designer, Hjalti Karlsson, took the opportunity to leave and start his own studio.) Initially, Sagmeister discovered that old patterns are hard to break. The start of his year off was delayed because he found it hard to say no to every client and ended up taking on pro bono projects. Once he got going, he structured his time carefully to ensure that he did not simply fill his days with chores. Some of his efforts were devoted to finding new ways of working. He read that the artist Robert Rauschenberg tries never to come into his studio with an idea. 'He says that if he does start with an idea, chances are he'll only come up with stuff that he or somebody else has done before him. He wants all the insecurities and doubts of the working process to become part of the final piece."[14] For a designer whose practice is based on starting from a strong idea, this was a completely foreign way of working. In a series of exercises, Sagmeister challenged himself to design a CD cover plus a 12-page booklet in just three hours, rather than the customary three months. This, too, yielded some unexpected directions that he would not otherwise have considered.

Sagmeister's year off came to an end in October 2001. He is doing less music-orientated work now and more 'cause-related' design, as well as corporate projects to pay the bills. The studio looks for clients whose agenda it shares. This includes the politically radical TrueMajority campaign – started by Ben Cohen, co-founder of Ben and Jerry's ice cream – which evolved from the Move Our Money initiative. Sagmeister tries to keep Friday mornings free to work on non-client-related ideas and 'little experiments', but admitted in 2002 that as far as self-initiated projects went – 'the ones that would really allow me to say something' – he had yet to achieve his goal. It may be that Sagmeister, like many designers, works most effectively when he can cooperate closely with clients whose values he believes in, people who will encourage him to use his interpretative skills at full stretch. If fame has a useful side, apart from gratifying the ego, it is that it acts as a magnet for the sophisticated collaborators on whom design's most telling and heartfelt moments so often depend.

THE SKIN CULT

Tattooing has become so widespread, fashionable and even common-place in the last decade that it is easy to forget how disreputable it used to be. Body adornment was vulgar. It was for sailors, criminals, gang members and lowlifes. In its most extreme forms, where people chose to cover their entire torsos and limbs with intricate designs, there was something of the freak show about it. For women, even more than for men, tattoos reeked of loose morals and a bad attitude. Prejudice maybe, but that is how it was.

The book *Modern Primitives*, published in 1989, revelled in the tattoo's outlaw status.[1] Along with piercing (which has also taken off) and scarification (still problematic for most of us), tattoos were seen as ways of exploring intense forms of experience through the body. Some disturbing images made the book controversial, but it played its part in the inexorable process by which tattoos moved from culture's edge to its heart. If that assimilation is now complete, celebrities can take much of the credit. A host of stars – Drew Barrymore, Christina Ricci, Ben Affleck – sport tattoos. Angelina Jolie has no fewer than 12, including the Latin words 'quod me nutrit me destruit' (that which nourishes me destroys me) below her navel next to a heavy black cross. The phrase comes from a 1585 portrait of the Elizabethan playwright Christopher Marlowe, where it appears on the canvas as a motto.

To judge by the number of weblogs devoted to it, many people are utterly fascinated by Jolie's gothic inscription. In aesthetic terms, it is quite different from the ornate but tacky illustrative style of the tradi-tional tattoo. Jolie seems here to be treating her body as the most inti-mate surface for writing, a public carrier for a personal manifesto of exceptional potency. A comparable, though even more extreme, fic-tional instance of this kind of body writing was the man with no long-term memory played by Guy Pearce in the thriller *Memento*. His flesh became a notepad on which he tattooed words he would not otherwise remember – an image pathetic to behold but also heroic in a way.

If florid, image-based tattoos are now so familiar as to seem rather obvious, verbal inscriptions are full of provocative potential. They also allow the wearer to make a statement through choice of typeface, moving tattoos away from the concerns of the tattoo artist and towards the established territory of graphic design. In 2003, New York writer Shelley Jackson, author of a story collection, *The Melancholy of Anatomy*, invited members of the public to participate in a new work titled 'Skin'. Jackson's idea is to inscribe each of the story's 2,095 words somewhere on the body of a complete stranger. If the word comes with a piece of punctuation attached, then that is also tattooed. The author

Shelley Jackson, author of *Skin*, 2004. Photograph: Frank Franklin II, AP sends a contract and a waiver, releasing her from responsibility, to those volunteers she accepts, and once the documents are signed she replies with a letter specifying the word. It is then up to the participant to obtain the tattoo and send her a photograph. A signed and dated certificate confirms participation in the work.

Jackson, a former art student, exerts just the right degree of typographic control. 'Tattoos must be in black ink and a classic book font,' she stipulates. 'Words in fanciful fonts will be expunged from the work.' As examples of acceptable typefaces, she suggests Caslon, Garamond, Bodoni and Times Roman. Courier is permissible and so are bookish sans serifs such as Futura or Gill Sans. 'Your tattoo should look like something to be read, not admired for its decorative qualities,' she advises. She has the title, 'Skin', tattooed in Baskerville on her wrist. On the Internet I found a photograph of the word 'swelling' – apt you might think – newly etched on a participant's ankle. The impact of the mysterious single word, with its imposingly sharp serifs, was quite different from a regular tattoo's.

By July 2005, 1,780 people had been accepted to take part in 'Skin' and there were more than 5,000 applications remaining to be processed. The words are assigned on a first-come, first-served basis in the sequence in which they appear in the story. Jackson describes her participants as 'words' and many will presumably wind up inscribed with nothing more exotic than 'and', 'the' or just 'a'. The full text will be known only to participants and it won't be made available in any other form. The words are free to communicate with each other and it seems likely that many will do so, but since their locations range from Birmingham, Alabama, to Brazil and Bangkok, a meeting of the entire narrative in one place is improbable. Groups of people are reported to have requested words in sequence so that they can form a sentence.

Some have already questioned whether 'Skin' can really be regarded as a text. You expect to be able to read a text, but this work is impenetrable to anyone outside its circle. The idea of a secret mark is certainly an essential element of many tattoos. Latin is rarely heard on Hollywood film sets, after all, and football superstars are not famed for their love of the classics. Yet David Beckham still felt it necessary to celebrate his shirt number with the words 'septem est perfectum' (seven is perfect) tattooed along his arm. Nine cast members from *The Lord of the Rings* symbolized their actorly bond by getting themselves tattooed with the words 'The Nine' – in Elvish.

'Skin' goes much further. It exists in intelligible though enigmatic fragments, as a tantalizing idea rather than as a reading experience. In that sense, it seems closer to conceptual art than to literature. It is possible that one of the words will break the vow of silence and leak the text, but while it lasts the project's exclusivity makes it highly appealing to participants. By agreeing to carry a mark on your body, you are granted access to the mystery; you become a cult member, an initiate. This goes a bit further than just following Nike chairman Phil Knight and other Nike staff and having a swoosh tattooed on your leg. Jackson swears she will attend the funerals of any words she outlives. The 'Skin' cult is for life and her work will gradually disappear with its guardians.

More of us than ever are adorning and modifying our bodies with tattoos, but the tattoo continues to serve the same purpose it always has – as a concentrated graphic expression of individuality and identity. The ways we go about expressing identity in other areas of life have evolved with the pressure of competition, and the tattoo must also evolve to keep pace. Stefan Sagmeister's image of himself needle-pointed with writing was an example of non-permanent scarification rather than tattooing, but viewers still recognized that marking your own tender skin is the most committed form of visual statement you can make. This kind of body-consciousness was mild compared to some of the piercings shown in *Modern Primitives*, but it was new in design practice.

It seems inevitable that body markings and graphic design will converge. It can only be a matter of time before people choose to embellish their flesh with personalized emblems and logos as well as typographic motifs created for their exclusive use by professional designers. A Sagmeister for the shoulder blade? A Bruce Mau for the buttock? A Paula Scher for the calf? The same devices could also be applied as personal branding to all kinds of non-bodily surfaces. In the case of public figures who are already marketed and perceived as brands, the possibilities for self-advertisement are endless.

FLESH SPEAKS

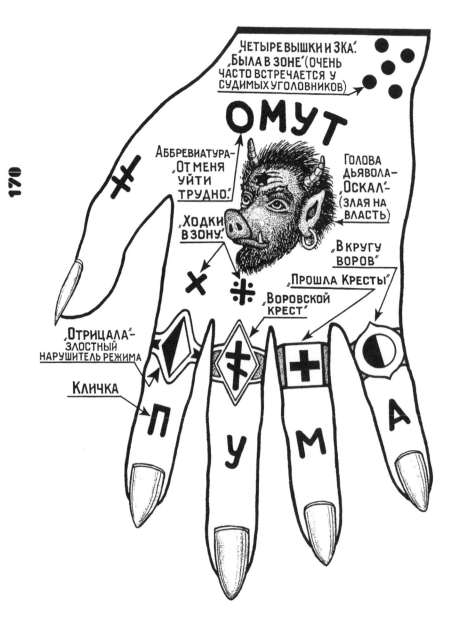

Finger-ring tattoos used by Russian women criminals. Illustration: Danzig Baldaev

Tattoos have become fashion accessories in recent years and there is no shortage of books about them. As a rule, these are not much more than cheaply produced picture collections bulging with colour pin-ups of men and women proudly displaying their body ornaments. *Russian Criminal Tattoo Encyclopaedia*, put together by the design team Fuel, takes a totally different approach.[1] Instead of large, obvious, paperback pages, it offers something much more concentrated and strange.

The book is a 400-page hardback not much bigger or heavier than a prayer book, with a traditional cloth binding and a thick, salmon-pink dust jacket. The title typeface, Berliner Grotesk, centred above a skull puffing on a fat cigar, makes the volume look like something published decades ago that has come to light in a dusty corner of a second-hand book shop. The encyclopaedia contains black-and-white photographs of Russian convicts by Sergei Vasiliev (the avoidance of colour signals its ambitions as a document), an essay by lexicographer and folklorist Alexei Plutser-Sarno, and a series of drawings of tattoos by Danzig Baldaev, who also contributes an introduction.

The style of the drawings, copied from criminals' bodies in jail, corrective labour colonies, isolation cells, public swimming pools, bathhouses and sometimes the morgue, is a cross between Mexican printmaker J.G. Posada and underground cartoonist Robert Crumb and the imagery is equally bizarre and often obscene. Baldaev, now in his seventies, has been collecting the tattoos since the 1940s when his father, a scholar accused by the state of being an enemy of the people, urged him to make a record of these antisocial markings so they would not be lost. The use of drawing imposes a graphically consistent style of presentation on the images and allows their iconography to be studied with greater attention. The book provides translations of the texts that feature in most tattoos, as well as information about a tattoo's meaning and sometimes additional details about the person it came from.

As *Russian Criminal Tattoo* convincingly reveals, this is a realm of unexpected graphic complexity. The tattoos are not mere decorations and there is nothing arbitrary about any of their elements. They are a form of speech and every symbol has a meaning that can be understood. A thief's entire biography can be written on the body in this way and, as Plutser-Sarno explains, the tattoos provide his bureaucratic documents – a complete 'service record' of achievements and failures, promotions and demotions, time spent in jail and 'transfers' to different types of 'work'. In the society of thieves, a man without tattoos has no social status. Tattoos are used to set out the rules and rituals of this hidden society, to regulate behaviour and maintain order. Any thief who tries to elevate his own position by misappropriating the tattoos of a 'legitimate thief' is likely to be killed and other kinds of false tattoo are forcibly excised from the body. Tattoos can also be imposed as a punishment, as a way of marking and degrading the wearer.

Many of the tattoos indicating a thief's background and position are worn like rings on the fingers. A crown in two rectangles denotes a criminal boss or 'authority'. An eight-pointed star in a circle means 'I became a thief because of poverty and a broken home'. Six dots indicate a convict at the lowest level of convict society, who acts as a servant to the criminal bosses. A rabbit means 'a lover of women' or 'a lover of group sex'. A heart in a rectangle indicates a despised convict with no status, such as a rapist.

Why are these images so fascinating to us? Plutser-Sarno argues that it is because the world of thieves long ago became the model for society as a whole. 'Our popular entertainers sing songs in criminal jargon, authors write entire novels in it, thousands of films are made about the criminal world, in which noble bandits "bump off" ignoble ones by the dozen or vice-versa.'[2] Criminal culture has infiltrated life far more completely than we grasp. This has special political resonance in Russia, but it is also true elsewhere. Although it has been assembled with care – you can't quite call it good taste – this book, too, is bound to be consumed as a fashion accessory, as its text freely admits. Still, it succeeds in presenting an often alarming glimpse of 'filth from our slavish past', as Baldaev puts it, and stands as an indictment of the state that created the brutal penal conditions in which this violent underworld found its soil.

CYBER BJÖRK

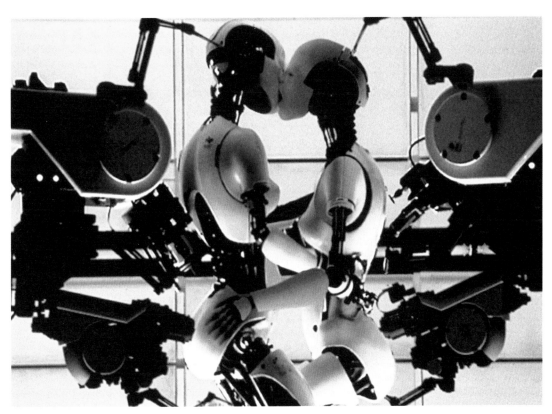

All is Full of Love,
pop video, 1998.
Director:
Chris Cunningham

If there is a single quality that defines the essence of the modern pop star, it is her ability to surprise the audience by constantly refreshing and remaking her public image. Most performers do this to some degree – clothes change, hairstyles evolve, old attitudes are cast off – but some of the most influential and durable stars project a sense that these continual transformations of appearance reflect revolutions of identity: that the artist, like her young audience, is engaged in a process of unceasing psychic experimentation and self-discovery. These are not merely costume changes, but an existential project in which the aim is to peel back the layers to expose new levels of inner reality. Stars who are unwilling or unable to perform these manoeuvres in the spotlight, preferring a single, possibly authentic but ultimately static image, run the risk of being regarded as all-too-predictable turns, for ever stuck in the aspic of their first success. We do not expect them to change and would be suspicious if they did, but nor do we look to them, as the years pass, for anything other than faintly nostalgic replays and a trip down memory lane.

Pop's first great ringmaster of the mutating self, still in many ways the template for those who followed, was David Bowie. Even before he became famous, Bowie was trying on different images for size: mod, hippie, Dylan-esque singer-songwriter. In 1971, as the Man Who Sold the World, he was a long-haired man-woman in a dress. Then came the 'leper messiah' Ziggy Stardust. Bowie was so obsessed with this persona that, by his own admission, he became hopelessly lost in the fantasy, staying in character when he was offstage, playing his 'mental games' with Ziggy so furiously that 'David Bowie' all but disappeared. Bowie extricated himself only to become a new creation, Aladdin Sane, a vivid red-and-blue lightning bolt slashed across his face. He followed this, soon after, with the urbane, icily detached figure of the Thin White Duke. This was not just play-acting. As Bowie explained in 1976, the constant urge to reinvent himself in public sprang from an enduring dissatisfaction with who he was and a 'superman'-like desire for self-enhancement. 'I wanted to make myself better. I always thought that I should change all the time ... I know for a fact that my personality is totally different to what it was then. I took a look at my thoughts, my appearance, my expressions, my mannerisms and idio-syncrasies and didn't like them. So I stripped myself down, chucked things out and replaced them with a completely new personality. When I heard someone say something intelligent, I used it later as if it were my own. When I saw a quality in someone that I liked, I took it. I still do that. All the time. It's just like a car ... replacing parts.'[1]

The sense that something vital was at stake for Bowie, that the image remakes were an almost involuntary reflex, was deeply compelling for the watching audience. Later stars who emerged in the 1980s described the liberating effect of seeing his concerts as teenage fans. From Boy George to Madonna, the sophisticated manipulation of self-image was now taken for granted as a crucial part of being a contemporary star. Madonna, in particular, took self-reinvention to the limit, unveiling a lavishly art directed new persona with every album or tour, from thrusting Material Girl to soulful New Age Earth Mother, and sometimes – as with her Marilyn Monroe look – playfully 'remixing' the iconic image of a bygone celebrity. For Madonna, too, these refits and makeovers were a game with identity. 'I just feel like I'm shedding layers,' she declared. 'I'm slowly revealing who I am.'[2] The star's body was both studio and mannequin, a display mechanism for her perpetual readjustments of hair, make-up, body shape, accessories, jewellery, clothing and style. Madonna modelled the look, the cameras recorded it, and the new image was reproduced on album sleeves and CD covers and broadcast around the world by promos and every other form of media.

If you were only to see the front covers of Björk's first three albums – *Debut*, *Post* and *Homogenic* – you might conclude that she was engaged in similar photographic revisions of her public identity. She began with a relatively direct image by Jean-Baptiste Mondino, most notable for the way that Björk, squarely facing the camera, seems to present herself with a hint of shyness or supplication in the way she raises her hands in prayer to her mouth. The second cover, shot by Stephane Sednaoui from the same point of view, is equally open and direct, but this time, in the airmail jacket (representing 'post') and vibrant background collage, there is considerably more artifice. By the third album, Björk – part empress, part geisha girl – is much more overt in using her own image (art directed by fashion designer Alexander McQueen) to symbolize the album's bleak lyrical themes. 'The songs are from a woman who was put in an impossible situation with as many restrictions as possible,' she explained. 'She becomes a warrior because of it. But she decides to fight back, not with weapons but with love.'[3] In Nick Knight's picture, Björk is cruelly constrained by neck rings, rendered handless by long fingernails and sightless by black contact lenses, and bound tightly at the waist. The image is not a fashion statement. It is a form of characterization, like an actor putting on the appropriate clothes to perform a part.

While Bowie or Madonna used their image changes to stage and express the drama of the self, the emphasis in Björk's collaboration with the designer Paul White, of Me Company, more often falls on the drama of the song. It could be likened, perhaps, to the difference between painting a self-portrait and using your own features as the basis of a portrait of someone else. The seeds of this approach were implicit in the *Debut* photo session, when White and Björk first began to talk about the various pictures in terms of the characters and stories in the lyrics. The cover design of 'Army of Me', a single taken from *Post*, showed just how free these interpretations would become. Björk is digitally transmuted to resemble the famous Japanese manga character Astro Boy (admired by both Björk and White) and on the back cover the image is multiplied to become the righteous 'army of me' that the unnamed figure addressed by the song will face if he or she doesn't stop complaining. In a related design for the single 'I Miss You', Björk once again appears as a digital character – still stylized but more recognizable as her – which was created by first sculpting a clay-fibre model, then scanning its coordinates into the computer.

For a significant star, already the subject of pubic fascination and attention in the press, this was a bold and unusual move to sanction. The pop star's charisma and power can be magnified to incalculable levels by the photographic image. 'For a pop singer or group,' writes Neil Tennant of the Pet Shop Boys, 'being photographed is a vital part of the pop process. The result can be a visual manifesto: this is what we are, what we want to be, where we're from and where we're going…'[4] These narcissistic images, lovingly created by stylists and lensmen, are the essential currency of fame. For fans, they function fetishistically as objects of adoration, envy, fantasy, longing and lust. They may be constructs, but they show the star's real skin, her eyes, her lips, her facial expressions and gestures; if you were there when the pictures were taken, you might even touch actual flesh.

In the 1970s, Bowie took a similar risk with his fleshly image only once, when he was painted as a sprawling canine with a human head for the cover of *Diamond Dogs*. For Björk, however, these body mutations are her usual way of operating. Her 'image' is just that – an image – and it has an increasingly virtual relationship to its point of origin. It may be that Björk, who has good reasons to fear public intrusion, is using these digital images as a kind of mask, a protective graphic persona, behind which she can live privately as herself. The digital Björks arrived at a time when there was much discussion in computer circles about the communicative potential of 'avatars' – simple digital characters, often cartoon-like, chosen to represent their users in online environments where the real person cannot be seen by others, a bit like a personal trademark. One of the attractions of using an avatar as an expression of individual identity is that you are in no way bound to it. You can change your image at will, or employ a whole gallery of avatars to convey different ideas and shades of mood. The possibilities for self-reinvention and exploring multiple identities are limitless.

Committed to a 'techno' sensibility – her word of highest approval – Björk enthusiastically embraces the computer's shape-shifting powers. White is frank in admitting that, for him, these designs are driven by the urge to discover how far the technology can be pushed. Their shared delight in playing interpretative games with her visual identity has generated some startling devices. For the 'Hyperballad' single, to visualize the song's image of the singer's body slamming into rocks at the foot of a cliff, White metamorphosed her head, using cyberscan data, into a stone. On 'Bachelorette', Björk appears once again to be merging with the natural world, as the garden reclaims her. 'She's trying to warn the garden about the dangers of civilisation,' notes White. 'What you are seeing is the wild animal inside the person who is on the cover.'[5] This theme of animalistic possession and mutation is given its most riveting expression in White's promo for 'Hunter'. It took nine or ten attempts to achieve the seamless take on which the transformation is based and the video's impact comes from the way it is constructed around Björk's electric presence as a performer. As she sings straight to camera, with naked shoulders and hairless head, silvery-blue shards seem to sprout from her skin. She shakes them off and continues, but they return, encroaching further than before. Once again she flicks them off, but soon her head and shoulders are completely encased by the features of a metallic future-tech bear. (It is not the first time Björk has had problems with bears. Michel Gondry's video for 'Human Behaviour' ends with a glimpse of her trapped inside a marauding fairy-tale bear's stomach.)

She continues to struggle and flex and succeeds in defeating the bear by forcing it to return inside her, where it doubtless lurks, waiting for its chance to re-emerge and take control once again. Using elemental imagery, painstakingly achieved with the most advanced modelling and rendering technology, 'Hunter' dramatizes the collision of techno and nature that lies at the heart of the singer's work. It captures the inner and outer struggle taking place within the real Björk, whose image is enhanced prosthetically and mediated by design.

Whatever the ending of 'Hunter' might suggest, in reality the cyborg Björk is in command. No matter how great her natural talent, her strategy of self-preservation is an entirely logical response to the relentless inspection of the media's gaze. 'A cyborg body is not innocent; it was not born in a garden; it does not seek unitary identity and so generate antagonistic dualisms without end (or until the world ends); it takes irony for granted,' writes Donna Haraway.[6] In the video for 'All Is Full of Love' (directed by Chris Cunningham) the cyborg-ing of Björk is made tenderly explicit, as the fully automated but still intensely soulful singer erotically embraces her cyborg lesbian lover – or perhaps, as with the earlier Isobel ('married to myself') it is an alternative version of herself. But what a self. Bowie talked about replacing bits of his personality like parts of a car. Here, everything is a replacement, delicately assembled and serviced by robotic arms and probes. The only recognizable parts of the singer (at a pinch) are the main features of her face. Björk has become software, the ghost in the media machine – as White's series of covers for the single 'Alarm Call', taken from *Homogenic*, also makes clear. Fields of impersonal white atoms stream over the star's face, shown in three different poses, defining its cyberscan contours, embodying its illusory presence, and Björk dissolves and disappears into phantasmal clouds of pure digital data.

FOLLOW YOUR BLISS

Even for those who follow his activities with interest, the news that Elliott Peter Earls was to be a designer in residence at Cranbrook Academy of Art, near Detroit – a post formerly held by the McCoys and the Makelas – came as something of a surprise. If ever a designer seemed like a certified oddball, pursuing a trajectory far removed from the obligations of institutional life, it is Earls. He is one of those unclassifiable, mutant blooms thrown up by the fractured landscape of 1990s design. My first encounter with his output came in 1993, when I was working on a survey of new design. A package of material from Cranbrook included several posters by Earls, who was in his final year. In one, an Astro Boy doll bursts through a sheet of glass, accompanied by the copy line, 'The side of my head hurts from thinking in the rain' – an announcement both engagingly direct in its physicality and intriguingly obscure in its state of mind.

The posters, he now reveals, represented something of a crisis. Earls was in the process of reinventing himself and, after that, things just got weirder. In 1995, operating as 'The Apollo Program', he released a CD-ROM, *Throwing Apples at the Sun*, which invaded the desktop and plunged viewers into a Supercard labyrinth of pop-up windows, sound effects, spoken-word pieces and Quicktime movies, as one layer led to the next. It was some kind of landmark in a medium that had mostly failed to deliver on its early promise, and reviewers were impressed. Around this time, Earls launched a triptych of deranged-looking typefaces – Dysphasia, Dysplasia and Dyslexia – that confirmed his gifts as a practitioner of outlandishly dysfunctional design. One could only wonder at the peculiar mind-space inhabited by their creator, who was apparently holed up in White Plains, somewhere outside of New York.

Emigre magazine promoted these projects and editor Rudy VanderLans, clearly a big fan of Earls, continued to feature his work, though a follow-up CD-ROM, *Eye Slingshot Lions*, was independently distributed. In 2002, in its latest guise as a CD, *Emigre* released Earls's first film, *Catfish*, on DVD, revealing yet another side to a figure for whom 'designer' seems an increasingly threadbare job description. Since 1998, Earls has given 40 or so live performances in which he delivers spoken texts, sings, acts, strikes attitudes, plays guitar, activates a number of self-made electronic contraptions, and uses computers to trigger a flow of random graphic imagery on big screens behind him. He has performed at Here, the Independent Art Center in New York; the Walker Art Center, Minneapolis; Fabrica in Treviso; Typo 2000 in Berlin; and the Maison des Arts et de la Culture in Créteil, France. 'If nothing pleases you about *Catfish*,' notes VanderLans pre-emptively, 'at least imagine the possibilities opened up by Earls's use and misuse of the different media he employs.'

Earls is a natural performer, intense and charismatic, with sculpted features and a wide mouth – imagine 'Wicked Game' singer Chris Isaak's slightly crazy brother. Watching him move around the stage with such authority, it is hard to believe he was in his thirties before it occurred to him to perform. He is tall, wiry and angular, a fast-talking, powerfully physical presence. His spacious studio at Cranbrook feels like a cross between a workshop and a film set, its floor littered with tripods, cables, gadgets and the audio rig he uses in performance. His banjo hangs on the wall.

At Jesuit high school in Cincinnati, Earls seems to have been one of the jocks. He was a committed athlete and soccer player with no interest in academic pursuits. It was his mother who suggested he turn his skills at drawing and painting into a career in graphic design. Assembling a portfolio with the help of an early mentor, he won a place at Rochester Institute of Technology in New York State. After graduating in 1988, he landed a job at de Harak and Poulin Associates in New York. Eleven months later, they fired him. 'I really didn't fit in there,' he says. 'It was a museum.' Mortified by this setback, Earls fled to

Greenwich, Connecticut, with his wife Darlene. At this stage he knew nothing about designers such as April Greiman and *Emigre*; he knew only about corporate design. Working at David Cundy Inc. in New Canaan, he finally saw an issue of VanderLans' increasingly influential type-zine. 'Bling! The light bulb went off over my head and I thought this was the most amazing thing I had ever seen.'

Earls decided to go to graduate school. Visiting Cranbrook for his interview, he fell in love with its bohemian, commune-like atmosphere. 'I believe in the mythology of the place and I think that was important. I believed in the McCoys. There was a process that I wanted to subject myself to. One of the things that was stressed by the McCoys and the visiting artists – Lorraine Wild and Ed Fella came while I was here – was that you have to take responsibility for the quality of your own education as well as your life.'

At Cranbrook, Earls started to question everything about himself, even his tastes in food. For those following in the footsteps of theory-hungry 1980s students such as Jeffery Keedy and Andrew Blauvelt, these were difficult times. 'I found I was rejecting a lot of the founding, underlying theoretical principles,' says Earls. 'I don't believe – as unacademic as this is going to sound – in the anti-teleological impulse. I don't believe in any of that shit. I believe there's an underlying order to the universe.' Earls's inquiry into values led him in some unlikely directions. He read Ayn Rand, Robert M. Pirsig's *Zen and the Art of Motorcycle Maintenance* and Jack Kerouac, subject of one of his Cranbrook posters. (There is a copy of *On the Road* on the shelf – it belongs to Darlene, who shares the studio.) Earls identified with Kerouac's call for a direct poetry of no abstractions, a joyful, Zen celebration of 'the true blue song of man'.

Earls's next attempt to function as a regular designer, at Elektra Records in New York, lasted only a few months. Asked to work on the Eagles' greatest hits for international release, he produced a cover design that was so 'country' in mood, it was clearly ironic. 'I simply could not bring myself to give them what they wanted,' he admits. Elektra returned the favour by showing him the door. These failures and the sense of futility were painful, but they helped Earls to focus; on the day he was fired, he sketched out a plan on his laptop for a multidimensional way of working that he has pursued ever since. His early grunge typefaces – best represented by the Dysphasia family – gave way to cleaner-edged, eccentrically cartoonish fonts such as Venus Diode, Typhoid Mary and Jig Saw Dropshadow, which feature heavily in his personal work. Under the influence of Edward Fella, drawing

Catfish, DVD by Elliott
Earls, Emigre, 2002

assumed increasing importance. 'You put the mark-making instrument to the page and you make beautiful or ugly or disgusting marks and you let them be true to themselves,' says Earls. His drawings, sometimes created with lo-fi scraperboard, have a repellent vigour. Their ungainly style, the very antithesis of fashionable digital illustration's purged and perfectionist linework, owes more to outsider art's brutal figuration and the unleashed id oozing from the darker kind of adult comic book. Earls surrounds his Picassoid, decapitated heads with graffiti-like annotations and unstable, aerobatic typography. In a sequence of images presented in *Emigre*, he offers portraits of four figures – Martin Luther King, Malcolm X, Max Ernst and Kurt Schwitters – whose ideas have 'left their mark on my soul'. His drawings, he says, are misinterpretations of the way Ernst drew.

In an *Emigre* essay, Earls lays out his intention to become a 'presumptive' designer – a term borrowed from Alvin Toffler's *The Third Wave* – positioned somewhere between traditional models of production and consumption. For Earls, this seems to translate into a goal of total self-sufficiency, a desire to become a twenty-first-century Renaissance man able to leap between disciplines with a single bound and somehow (this part is unclear) escape the dilemma of a pluralistic environment in which everything is possible and nothing taboo. Of course, the desire not to be constrained by disciplinary boundaries has been a cultural ideal in recent years, to the point of cliché, though few have what it takes to become a convincing multidisciplinary artist. Whatever one thinks of his aesthetic, Earls possesses an unusual array of talents and an enviable facility to acquire new skills. He taught himself guitar as a student at Cranbrook, composed songs, picked up practical electronics, wrote a screenplay, and can do almost anything he wants with a computer. In *Catfish*, he delivers an impressively obnoxious performance as a buck-toothed, hillbilly typeface-salesman – as a performer and actor, he sometimes seems to tap into a deep well of inner rage.

Earls's work has undeniable power and he has succeeded in finding audiences outside the insular club of design. If he presented himself purely as an artist or musician, one probably would not even feel the need to ask: what does it all mean? Or, if one were to ask this, it would come some way behind the immersive experience of the work itself. In recent years, many design projects have aspired to be absorbed in this way, but design's long-standing, disciplinary commitment to 'communication' means the spectre of meaning can never be entirely repressed. Nevertheless, Earls's work resists interpretation. 'The program's construction reinforces the theme of intellectual dyslexia,' notes Kenneth FitzGerald, discussing *Throwing Apples*. 'Fragments fail to coalesce to definite meaning, nor do they attempt to.' If Earls's creations were less persuasive on an experiential level, one might dismiss them by saying that he is merely 'expressing himself'. However, Earls continues to view what he does as being firmly based on design principles, even though artists, film-makers, musicians and writers use similar compositional principles without calling them 'design'.

His own reflections on meaning are distinctly inward-looking. While he was a student at Cranbrook, he saw tapes of Joseph Campbell and Bill Moyers's PBS television series *The Power of Myth*. One programme dealt with Hindu concepts of perfect consciousness, perfect being and perfect bliss. 'Man's purpose in life is to attain those things,' says Earls. 'Perfect bliss is the easiest one to understand. You follow your bliss. So in my work the point is self-actualization, to figure out exactly who I am.... These [works] are the visual records of the attempt to follow that sense of being at home with the work. In Buddhism, they refer to it as the white moment, where time and space collapse.' Earlier, Earls had spoken of the quest for something transcendent in Kerouac's view of poetry; here he invokes the idea of the sublime. He wants to create something 'deeply human' that would elicit emotion from the viewer. 'I guess part of this is trying to figure out what those structures are, to try to illuminate the beauty, the horror, the terror and the poetry of life.' These ideas are familiar enough in art and poetry, ancient and new, but it is unusual to hear a designer express them.

Like others in search of the contemporary sublime, Earls uses multifocal complexity to provoke a vertiginous sense of displacement. He wants to make the strange familiar and the familiar strange. He cites Dick Hebdige's essay about Talking Heads' *The Road to Nowhere* video, where Hebdige discusses the tendency in pop videos to substitute referential density for narrative coherence.[1] *Throwing Apples* was Earls's *Road to Nowhere* and he confesses to once replacing Byrne's name with his own in the text. By the end of Talking Heads' clip, four alternative image-tracks are running in separate picture-in-picture boxes over the main image. More recently, Earls has come round to the view that the degree of referential density in the *Eye Slingshot Lions* show is sometimes overwhelming. Looking out into the audience in the middle of a non-linear poetry rap that verged on nonsense, he would see blank stares. 'Anytime there was any kind of narrative strain at all, all of a sudden the audience would be with me.' Earls is operating in a genre of experimental music/performance that includes the likes of the

Residents and Laurie Anderson. My guess is that if he were to shed the 'design' tag, find a manager and develop his grasp of narrative and character, he would have a show that, while still challenging, could achieve much bigger audiences.

By taking on the responsibility of 2D designer in residence at Cranbrook, Earls seems to be seeking to challenge himself: it would be easier to work alone. It is almost inevitable that his concerns will underscore a self-absorbed view of the designer as aspiring artist for which some have criticized Cranbrook. 'The first and most important step is to be true to one's self,' Earls writes. 'To allow one's work to be "true," to be "honest," to be "real" even in deceit.'[2] (But why those inverted commas? Are these ideals not attainable? Is their display some form of pretence?) 'Students must realize the importance of risk within work,' he adds. 'They must realize that approval seeking is a vicious cycle that never leads to truly powerful work.'[3] As an educational credo, this will only take a designer so far, but in his own case, it has definitely been the making of him. Graphic design may yet prove to be the least of it.

APPLY FOR AN UPGRADE TODAY

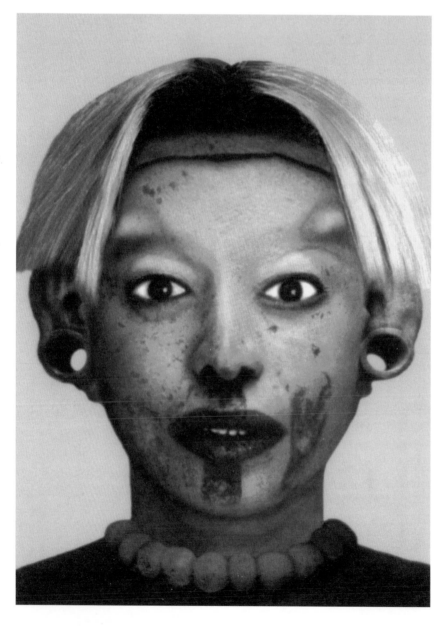

Refiguration/Self-Hybridation # 30, cibachrome print by Orlan, 1999

As we move into the twenty-first century, it becomes ever clearer that the ultimate, most intimate territory for design is not electronics, or interiors, or furniture, or the Web. It is us – our own living, breathing, biological selves. People are accustomed now to expect the highest standard of design in shops, restaurants, hotels, cars and every kind of product for the home or office. We are surrounded by immaculate surfaces, so it was perhaps inevitable that the epidermal imperative to polish, restyle, enhance and upgrade would extend to our own flesh. Appearances matter more than ever, we are constantly told. If so, the personal makeover has become our most fundamental design task.

Of course, people have always tried to make the best of themselves. Cosmetic surgery has been around for decades, but public acceptance of it is growing all the time. Between 1982 and 1992, according to the American Academy of Cosmetic Surgeons, approval increased by 50 per cent among those surveyed. On TV, plastic surgery has now become mass entertainment, with reality shows such as ABC's *Extreme Makeover* and Fox's *The Swan* commanding audiences of 8 million or 9 million, despite cries of misogyny. *The Swan* was such a hit that a second series began in October 2004.

On the show, 16 women agree to isolate themselves from home and family for three months while a team of eight experts – a life coach, a therapist, two cosmetic surgeons, a cosmetic dentist, a laser eye surgeon, a dermatologist and a fitness trainer – go to work on every personal attribute of these 'ugly ducklings' that they consider less than perfect. A mother of five submitted to a brow lift, a cheek lift, work on her upper and lower eyelids, and leg liposuction. The surgeons added extra skin to the tip of her nose, injected collagen into her lips, implanted new teeth, augmented her breasts and gave her a stomach tuck. At the end of this gruelling overhaul the women competed in pairs to see who would go through to the final pageant and be crowned.

The Swan is breathtakingly presumptuous and exploitative. It normalizes the idea that perfectly ordinary variations in appearance should be expunged. It turns therapy into competition, promising enhancement only to insist that 15 out of 16 women are not good enough to win. It reinforces the 'Barbie doll' ideal of female attractiveness, which will do nothing to help the self-image and self-esteem of younger viewers who do not conform to this media-determined stereotype.

Yet *The Swan* is riveting because, in its ruthlessly brutal way, it exposes the extent to which the desperate urge to redesign ourselves has taken hold in our culture. Many people nurse deep feelings of inadequacy about aspects of their appearance – it is as moving as it is uncomfortable to hear the women reveal this anguish on the pro-gramme. Now, if you have the money – or a TV station prepared to pay – you can do something about it. It has been suggested that the increas-ing popularity of cosmetic surgery is a sign that beauty is becoming democratized – it is no longer the province of the super-rich. Why should those who are genetically fortunate enjoy all the advantages that accrue to the naturally good-looking while others miss out? With judi-cious use of the surgeon's knife, we can take control of our appearance and increase our chances.

One of the most revealing explorations of this new set of values comes in the shape of the American television drama *Nip/Tuck*. The series follows the fortunes of two successful plastic surgeons, Sean McNamara and Christian Troy. The partners enjoy designer lifestyles, operate in stylish blue gowns, and every surgical procedure, shown in gory close-up for our amusement, begins with a CD being inserted into a state-of-the-art upright CD player. Troy is a shallow, narcissistic sex addict and attends a sexaholics meeting. One episode begins with him admiring the sleek, erotic contours of a yellow Lamborghini he would like to buy. He proposes a company making porn films to McNamara as a lucrative source of new business. The surgeons will carry out ten implants, liposuctions and reductions on porn stars every month. McNamara, a more scrupulous family man, objects. 'Take off your judgemental blinders, Sean,' says Troy. 'The line that divides the porn industry and plastic surgery is a thin one. We are both selling fantasy, aren't we?'[1]

Eventually, Troy changes his mind about operating on porn stars, while a more corrupt plastic surgeon colleague, Merrill Bobolit, who we encounter draped with nubile women by his outdoor pool, wins the porn star contract. Troy even takes the Lamborghini back to the show-room. 'This car tells the whole world who you've become,' says the baffled salesman. 'Which is why I'm returning it,' replies Troy.[2] Yet the programme's unvarying menu of loveless sex, frivolous surgical alter-ation and empty designer perfection tells a different story, whatever morals the characters are made to spout. In this world, there really isn't much difference between the fantasies expressed by the porn industry and those expressed by cosmetic surgery.

Even real cosmetic surgeons betray contradictory views of their calling. In a book called *Aesthetic Surgery*, aimed at readers with an interest in the subject's cultural aspects, 18 of the world's most renowned plastic surgeons answer questions about their motivations and attitudes to beauty, ageing and sex, and the future of cosmetic surgery. Some surgeons are almost sentimental in their insistence that beauty is more than skin-deep. 'The most beautiful part of a person is inside,' says one. 'I believe that inner beauty will ultimately prevail over external beauty,' says another. 'Beauty only exists in the eye of the beholder, after all,' says a third.[3] Be that as it may, all the surgeons have flourishing careers tending to the wishes and whims of patients who believe that something more than inner beauty is required for their personal happiness. The book shows photos of Iranian women who sought nose jobs for normal noses, Chinese people who have endured the agony of surgical leg extension, a boy whose perfectly ordinary ears were resculpted and pinned back at his parents' request, and a good-looking, 20-year-old Japanese male who was nevertheless dissatisfied and wanted Caucasian features. The aim is often to look more Western.

Most of the surgeons are unreservedly upbeat in their view of cosmetic surgery's possibilities, but every so often a less ebullient and perhaps more realistic assessment of its social future emerges. Dr Serdar Eren, head of the Center for Aesthetic Plastic Surgery in Cologne, believes that people will increasingly invest in their appearance instead of their emotional well-being – an 'unfortunate development' in his view.[4] Dr Hans-Leo Nathrath, head physician at the Department of Plastic Surgery at the Arabella Clinic, Munich, notes: 'Aesthetic surgery will become like a popular sport – which will also have negative repercussions. The gap between the rich and the poor will continue to widen, and medical ethics will need to address this.' He hopes that 'the elites of Europe will continue to favour a natural concept of beauty'.[5]

The most subversive remarks come from Dr Dai Davis, director of the Institute of Cosmetic and Reconstructive Surgery in London. 'In many ways, beauty is a form of tyranny,' he says. 'Unfortunately, society places far too much importance on beauty.'[6] One could hardly have put it better, but cosmetic surgery is increasingly regarded as just another aspect of our everyday health, fitness and beauty regimes. In 2005, the women's magazine *Top Santé* introduced a regular plastic surgery section, 'Nip & Tuck', alongside the usual stories about slimming, dealing with stress and feeling decades younger.[7] 'Lose 10 Years with Our Extreme Makeover!' promised the cover. Inside, 47-year-old Margaret Tippins described her liposuction and *Top Santé* invited readers who fancied a restorative visit to the plastic surgeon to send in their stories and photos. The magazine would pick up the tab for the procedure for the chosen few.

The time is fast approaching when it will be possible to redirect destiny's path at an even more fundamental level. A book about genetic engineering by Dr Gregory Stock, director of the Program on Medicine, Technology and Society at the University of California at Los Angeles (UCLA), spells out the goal in its title: *Redesigning Humans.*[8] Stock argues that the scientific developments that will ultimately lead to 'human biological design' are already so far advanced that nothing can be done to stop the ability we shall soon possess to manipulate our babies' genes, influencing their health, looks and abilities, and helping them live longer. This is our future. The design of outer perfection will be achieved by God-like acts of inner correction.

These may not be developments that designers follow closely, but it is striking how the language used in cosmetic surgery and biological research is informed by the same aesthetic values and design terminology that pervade our design culture. Dr Keizo Fukuta, chief surgeon at Verite Clinic in Tokyo, compares himself to an interior designer: 'Painters and sculptors create their works from scratch; an interior designer, on the other hand, needs to work with the architecture, the budget and the client's taste. My work process is akin to this – I similarly take the ideas and possibilities offered by my clients and optimise them aesthetically.'[9]

Behind so much of this speculation lies a desire to transcend the limits of the body, to overcome its perceived design flaws and weaknesses, and ultimately, to prolong life itself. The wilder fringes of this world are inhabited by artificial intelligence thinkers, transhumanists and 'extropians' who dream of downloading human intelligence and making themselves immortal. Natasha Vita-More, an artist and bodybuilder, has collaborated with a team that includes AI heavyweights such as Marvin Minsky and Hans Moravec to create a prototype of a technologically enhanced future body called Primo.

'I love fashion,' Vita-More told *Wired.* 'Our bodies will be the next fashion statement; we will design them in all sorts of interesting combinations of texture, colors, tones, and luminosity.'[10] Vita-More evokes her Primo 'designer body' in the promotional language of consumer design: 'What if your body was as sleek, as sexy, *and* felt as comfortable as your new automobile?... Primo's radical body design is more powerful, better suspended and more flexible ... offering extended performance and modern style.'[11] Where the twentieth-century human body makes mistakes, wears out, usually has a single gender and is capable of only a limited lifespan, twenty-first-century Primo's post-human superbody features an error-correction device, can be upgraded and change gender, and is potentially ageless. Our sense of humanity –

missing, you might think, from this cyborg fantasy – will be superseded by an 'enlightened transhumanity', whatever that might be.

As an unusual contribution to the debate surrounding some of these issues, the British industrial design team Dunne & Raby undertook a self-initiated research project, partly funded by the Design Institute at the University of Minnesota. Their illustrated report, *Consuming Monsters*, describes BioLand, a notional place in the near future that allows them to explore how biotechnology might flow from laboratories, through the consumer landscape, and into our homes, using a range of hypothetical products and services. We have a tendency to deal with some of these issues – designer babies, consumer eugenics, DNA theft – in terms of philosophical and moral abstractions. Dunne & Raby want to make the issues concrete and easier to visualize by embodying them in actual things. 'Ideas of right and wrong are not just abstractions,' they say. 'They are entangled in everyday consumer choices.'[12]

In a vision worthy of maverick sci-fi film-maker David Cronenberg, Dunne & Raby use projects by themselves and other designers to investigate a society of BioBanks, DNA detection, sperm guns for artificial insemination, utility pigs for growing replacement body parts, genetic-code copyright certificates, pheromone furniture polish and clone counselling. They also make a startling prediction. In the future, they suggest, 'beauty deflation' will occur.[13] We will grow tired of a world of generically good-looking designer people and genetic technology will be used to emphasize the physical features, racial characteristics and family traits we once thought it necessary to suppress.

It's going to be a long time coming.

WHAT'S THE MATTER WITH US?

I have to admit I got it wrong with Paul Davis. My aim was to write an essay about British designers' favourite artist/illustrator, rather than a profile, but I decided to go and see him anyway to pick up information about his way of working. I planned to maintain a polite, professional distance, but Davis is friendly and sociable, with a way of pulling you into his world. He enjoys food, drinking, telling stories, hanging out, and he wanted to go for lunch, so we did. He spoke freely, with great warmth, and I concluded this first meeting with the sense that he would probably make an exceptionally communicative interviewee. Perhaps an interview-based profile was the best way of tackling this, after all. Still, I wanted to write something more discursive.

We made another date to meet. This time he was edgy. The prospect of a more formal, tape-recorded interview seemed to rattle him. My main concern was finding somewhere quiet enough to make a good recording, and we wound up in a dark-brown, dimly lit ante-room, like something out of a David Lynch film, in a bar near to his studio in Curtain Road, east London. With the tape running, Davis was an odd mixture of volubility and slightly awkward reticence. It was hard to glean much detail about his intentions as an artist – he would say two or three short sentences and then clam up. But in other more private and emotional matters, which I hadn't asked about, he was almost too forthcoming, though I couldn't help admiring his openness and generosity of spirit.

I emerged not much the wiser about his methods, but with my impressions of his work, as I had first perceived it, deflected, if not compromised, by my growing awareness of the man. I had lost my detachment. After such generosity, how could I be anything other than generous in return? I had even heard his view of critics – 'a really horrible way of living'. This didn't appear to be personal, but being treated as an exception only made it worse.

'I DON'T GIVE A DAMN ABOUT FAME AND ALL THAT SHIT.'

Davis was born in Paulton, Somerset, in 1962. He graduated from Exeter College of Art and Design in 1985, but it was more than a decade before he made much headway. In the late 1980s, he worked mainly in collage, then the dominant approach in illustration. The high point came in 1988 when he exhibited a series of personal pieces created with David O'Higgins in a show titled 'Spanking Britain'. The 25 collages, Davis explained at the time, reflected disillusionment with design, the media, popular culture, fashion, the financial sector, postmodern housing in the Docklands and the invention of the yuppie. He subsequently abandoned collage, realizing that he would much sooner draw, but found himself churning out undemanding magazine illustrations to order. The sense of disenchantment remained.

In 1996, it occurred to Davis that constant seasonal change meant that there might be a future in fashion illustration and he showed a collection of images to Jo Dale at the *Independent on Sunday*'s Sunday Review. Dale commissioned a series of full-page watercolours illustrating clothes and accessories by Gucci, Chanel, Calvin Klein and Paul Smith. Some of Davis's later traits were already evident: random scribbles, figures floating against nebulous backgrounds and a kind of studied clumsiness, as though the artist was drawing less well than he could. Within days, Harvey Nichols had approached Davis to create an 11-window display to promote the menswear department at its Knightsbridge store, while Sir Terence Conran, also thinking big, ordered up a 24-metre (80-foot) mural for his new Bluebird restaurant in Chelsea. By the end of the 1990s, Davis was collaborating with British art director Tony Arefin in New York on IBM's Magic Box campaign, his biggest, most lucrative project to date.

He continues to work for some high-profile commercial clients – ads for Virgin Atlantic, an annual review for Channel 4 – but these illustration projects display a softer, more pliable, more decorative side.

Davis understands design, appears to get on well with designers and is sympathetic to their aims, but like many who straddle the art/design divide, it is clear that the work that matters to him most allows him to record his experiences and reactions without compromise. These more personal pieces have won him attention. The commercial projects trade off the Davis charisma with some charm, but if they were the sum total of his output we would not be talking about him.

'I'M JUST A NOSY BASTARD.'

Davis seems most himself when, on the page, he is doing very little. A drawing of a surfer, from a series of ten, is as spare and mysterious as a haiku. Davis captures the essential features of the man's face with just a few shaky outlines and scribbles. The eyes seem unfocused: he is lost in a world of his own. The stubble on his chin suggests his casual lifestyle and the sideburn proclaims 'dude'. 'I'm so far outside normal society' says the hand-lettered copy line over his head. Above that, Davis has written 'A surfer explains' and this small addition is vital. We would have no idea without it who the man is, but it also establishes a context for his disaffection. He evidently sees himself as part of a special group, living by an alternative code. His remark implies that 'normal society' could never understand him, yet he looks spaced out and not entirely there. There is an unmistakable note of irony in Davis's scene-setting. The man is clearly kidding himself. He isn't the bold, socially radical surf hero he imagines himself to be.

One final element of the image is also typical of Davis's work. The drawing has been made on a narrow-ruled notepad, with a torn top edge and crossed-out elements left as they stand. The picture may or may not have been created in situ (on a beach? in a bar?) but the notepaper adds a feeling of immediacy, informality and verisimilitude. Davis might have made up this surfer character, but the sketch has the air of something seen and heard and faithfully transcribed, like a visual report.

This is how he operates. The people in his pictures seem real because usually they are real. He interrogates friends and acquaintances. He listens in on conversations in bars and restaurants – 'Yes, my husband's penis is rather small' – and overhears moments of unfortunate candour and self-revelation in the street: 'Fuck off. Of course I love you.' He approaches complete strangers in hotel lobbies, asks them impertinent questions and makes a careful note of what they say. His likeable manner sets his subjects at ease and they allow him to get in close. In some ways, Davis works exactly like a journalist with note-

Product Revamp Director, drawing by Paul Davis, 2004

book in hand, looking for clues to what people are thinking about now and what makes them tick. His drawings may be reduced to a few simple elements, offering the viewer a deceptively quick hit, but he has an unerring ability to delineate – and flay – a personality with a few incisive strokes. He can do this with graphite, coloured pencil, ink or paint. These faces are both characters and types. We feel we know people like this.

'I'M MISANTHROPIC. I CAN'T HELP IT.'
The bleakness of Davis's view is alleviated by humour, but its prevailing colour is black. His characters are empty vessels: ignorant, foolish, self-centred, deluded and boring. Davis returns repeatedly to sex and relationships (with the emphasis on sex), to the self-aggrandizing folly of the business world and to the general emptiness of it all – in one drawing even bullshit comes in a Liquitex tube. 'I think new media is fascinating' observes a talking potato head, a minimal figure even by Davis's usual standards. *God Knows*, a collection of his drawings, introduces us to a grinning Director of Global Sloganeering and an equally shifty Product Revamp Director – their ponderous job titles are comment enough.[1] In *Blame Everyone Else*, Davis scratches out the golden tresses of yet another jargon-spouting new media lackey: 'D'you realise that cross-platform sharing has been a reality for some time now, as has multi-tasking, living brands, resonant messaging and many more' she inquires, her empty words occupying far more space than her own image. Another small, bowed figure appears to be afflicted by almost every malaise that modern life can throw at a person: 'Bankrupt, overdrawn, credit blacklisted, lonely and terminally ill.'[2]

Davis has been described as a satirist, but he dislikes the term. Nor does he regard himself as a moralist, though he admires William Hogarth, who certainly was. He takes issue with the suggestion that his work criticizes the world, even though this is what it does. Davis prefers to describe his output as a 'reflection' of what he sees, and himself as a 'misanthropist'. When I pointed out that the definition of misanthropy – a little-used word these days – was hatred of the human race, he denied that it meant this. As a self-declared 'beauty-ist' and life-loving romantic, he seems to interpret misanthropy as the stance of someone struggling with dismay at the way people so often fall short of their potential to live good lives, behave decently and tell the truth.

Here I run into problems because, while I can accept this statement of intention after becoming acquainted with the man, it certainly wasn't quite how I read the work before I met him. Davis's drawings are unsentimental and unsparing, often to the point of cruelty. His most sustained feat of reporting and concentrated jet of bile is the book *Us & Them*, documenting what the British think of the Americans and the Americans think of the Brits.[3] Davis's caustic ear for self-serving nonsense and fatuous opinions delivered in tones of great authority is pitch perfect and the acid flows from his pen. 'There's a certain "old school" arrogance. AH HATE IT!' shrieks a woman he encounters in a Chicago hotel. From the way Davis draws her, with desiccated body, face screwed tight in fury and ropes of hair hanging down to the floor, it is hard to believe that the loathing is not mutual. In many ways, the ostensible theme of the book, transatlantic misperceptions, seems like no more than a pretext. *Us & Them*'s real subject, and it is Davis's abiding concern, is the fallibility and delusion that is part of our human nature, wherever we happen to live.

'I CAN'T HELP MAKING PICTURES. IT'S ALMOST NOT MY FAULT.'
A number of striking image-makers have come to the fore in recent years, but Davis is top of the heap. He was voted 'best illustrator working today' by readers of *Creative Review* in 2002. Why do people like his work so much? It has an attitude, a spark of ruthlessness, that most colleagues lack and, in some crucial respects, it is totally in tune with the times. The maladjusted weirdness of ordinary people has become a staple of alternative British television comedy. Programmes such as *The League of Gentlemen*, Chris Morris's *Jam*, *Little Britain*, *Green Wing* and *Nighty Night* parade a gallery of dysfunctional characters: self-fixated but lacking in self-awareness, emotionally incontinent but unable to make a real connection, sociopathic to the point of depravity. Oddball TV reporter Louis Theroux and outrageous chat show host Graham Norton encourage members of the public to expose themselves for our entertainment. No foible, obsession, bodily function, act of unpleasantness or sexual mishap is so private, embarrassing or shameful that it can't be mined for a laugh.

But what, we might ask, is the underlying purpose of the joke? Is it the satisfaction of seeing social taboos broken? A therapeutic moment of recognition that something true but previously unstated has been revealed, allowing us to go forward as better-adjusted human beings? Or a darker, less wholesome kind of pleasure in prurience and humiliation for their own sakes? Whatever his intentions, many of Davis's drawings exhibit much the same fascination with areas of experience that were once off-limits to popular culture.

I'LL ALWAYS, ALWAYS LOVE YOU

He is at his most ambivalent when he deals with sex. The primeval, clay-like men and women displaying their genitals in *Lovely* look deeply uneasy, with their eyes popping out of their heads.[4] The volume numbers written on the pictures and the printed grids used as backgrounds add to the perception that they are specimens for study. Davis might be showing us how these people have chosen to objectify and demean themselves by assuming porn poses, or he might just be saying: look, this is how we humans are, isn't it ridiculous and, let's be honest, rather funny? Then again, it is possible that Davis really doesn't know quite what he means by some of these sexual images. When I asked him about it in the gloom of the David Lynch bar, the only answer he came up with, delivered as though nothing more needed saying, was 'I love sex'.

'I HAVE NEVER FOUND MY VOICE. THAT'S THE BEAUTY OF IT.'
Meeting Davis certainly complicated my sense of his work. I had him pegged as exactly the kind of person that he says he is: a misanthropist. Now he strikes me as more like a disappointed idealist. It is socially unwise to make moral rulings about other people's behaviour today – what gives us the right? Often, though, as in the surfer portrait, there can be little doubt about what Davis thinks of his subjects. He dares to make a judgement. David Carson, famous as a surfer, commissioned the surfer pictures for *Big* magazine in 2001, but rejected them all as too negative, according to Davis. Clearly the drawings had made their point a little too effectively.

At other times, a Davis image could be saying almost anything. What does his 'modernist vagina building' inscribed on MetaDesign's letterhead mean? Or the two soft toys hanging by their ears from a washing line? He would probably relish this ambiguity, since he likes the idea of a critical response that circles endlessly around the subject, opening up further lines of inquiry without reaching a firm conclusion. But this is the dominant approach in most criticism today (as distinct from evaluative reviewing) and it could be seen as a failure of nerve, a sign of moral exhaustion that cannot be reconciled with a world view as passionately committed as Davis's. 'Being a romantic,' he says, 'you are bound to be let down.' His drawings propose one thing with indelible conviction. It's not just everyone else who is to blame. It's all of us.

I'll Always, Always Love You, **drawing by Paul Davis, 2003**

NOTES

INTRODUCTION

1   Quoted in Rachel Bell, 'It's Porn, Innit?',
    Guardian, G2, 15 August 2005, p. 6.
2   Louise Evans of W.H. Smith quoted in,
    'It's Porn, Innit?', p. 6.
3   Christina Valhouli, 'The Naked Truth',
    I.D., April 2001, pp. 62-7.
4   Clare Dowdy, 'Style (and Size) Matter',
    Design Week, 8 September 2005, pp. 18-19.
5   Angharad Lewis, 'Brazen Images', *Grafik*,
    August 2003, p. 39.
6   Caroline Roberts, editorial, *Grafik*, November
    2003, p. 3.
7   Heseon Park, 'The Playground', *Colors*,
    no. 64, spring 2005, pp. 28-33.
8   Quoted in Rowan Pelling, 'A Bisexual Table,
    Please', *Guardian*, G2, 27 July 2005, p. 10.
9   Steven Marcus, *The Other Victorians:
    A Study of Sexuality and Pornography in
    Mid-Nineteenth Century England*, London:
    Weidenfeld and Nicolson, 1966, p. 216.
10 Ibid., p. 242.
11 Ibid., p. 154.
12 Judith Williamson, 'Sexism with an Alibi',
    Guardian, 31 May 2003. For a longer version of
    the essay, see 'Retro-Sexism', *Eye*,
    no. 48 vol. 12, summer 2003, pp. 44-53.

HYPHENATION NATION

1   Bruce Mau, *Life Style*, London: Phaidon,
    2000, pp. 41-3.
2   Ibid., p. 43.
3   Ibid., p. 45.
4   Ibid.

5   Jonas Ridderstråle and Kjell Nordström,
    Funky Business: Talent Makes Capital Dance,
    London and New York: Pearson Education,
    2002 (first published 2000), p. 135.
6   Ibid., p. 143.
7   Ibid., p. 144.
8   Jeremiah Creedon, 'Seller's Market',
    Utne Reader, December 1999, p. 52.
9   Bidisha, 'Show Me the Money',
    Dazed & Confused, October 2000.
10 Alice Rawsthorn in *We Shape the Things
    We Build, Thereafter They Shape Us*,
    Caterpillar brochure, 1999.
11 Steve Slocombe, 'It's a Sell-Out', *Sleazenation*,
    October 2001, p. 5.
12 Ryan Mathews and Watts Wacker, 'Deviants,
    Inc.', *Fast Company*, March 2002, p. 76. See also
    Ryan Mathews and Watts Wacker, *The
    Deviant's Advantage: How Fringe Ideas Create
    Mass Markets*, London: Random House, 2002.
13 'Sponsor's Foreword' in Jennifer Mundy (ed.),
    Surrealism: Desire Unbound, London: Tate
    Publishing, 2001, p. 6.
14 Morris Berman, *The Twilight of American
    Culture*, London: Duckworth, 2000, p. 99.
15 Tibor Kalman, 'Fuck Committees (I Believe in
    Lunatics)' in Peter Hall and Michael Bierut (eds),
    Tibor Kalman: Perverse Optimist, New York:
    Princeton Architectural Press, 1998.
16 Thomas Frank, 'Half Empty', *Artforum*,
    February 1999, pp. 26-8.
17 *Life Style*, p. 39.
18 See Mark Kingwell, 'Interior Decoration:
    Politics as Lifestyle Accessory', *Harper's*

Magazine, June 2001, pp. 72-5; and Hal Foster, 'Hey, That's Me', *London Review of Books*, 5 April 2001, pp. 13-14.

19 Quoted in Rob Lieber, 'Creative Spaces', *Fast Company*, January 2001, p. 142.

20 Rem Koolhaas, Miuccia Prada and Patrizio Bertelli, *Projects for Prada Part 1*, Milan: Fondazione Prada Edizioni, 2001.

MEET ME AT THE CHECKOUT

1 Chuihua Judy Chung, Jeffrey Inaba, Rem Koolhaas and Sze Tsung Leong (eds), *Harvard Design School Guide to Shopping*, Cologne: Taschen, 2001.

2 Chuihua Judy Chung, Jeffrey Inaba, Rem Koolhaas and Sze Tsung Leong (eds), *Great Leap Forward*, Cologne: Taschen, 2001.

3 *Harvard Design School Guide to Shopping*, p. 134.

4 Rem Koolhaas, 'Junkspace' in *Harvard Design School Guide to Shopping*.

5 Ibid.

LUXURIOUS FRUGALITY

1 David Brooks, *Bobos in Paradise: The New Upper Class and How They Got There*, New York: Simon and Schuster, 2000, p. 42.

THIS MONTH'S COVER

1 Quoted in Jeremy Leslie, *Issues: New Magazine Design*, London: Laurence King Publishing, 2000, p. 44.

2 See, for instance, Ros Ballaster, Margaret Beetham, Elizabeth Frazer and Sandra Hebron, *Women's Worlds: Ideology, Femininity and the Woman's Magazine*, London: Macmillan, 1991.

3 See Michael Koetzle (ed.), *Twen: Revision einer Legende*, Munich and Berlin: Klinkhardt & Biermann, 1995.

4 See David Hillman, Harri Peccinotti and David Gibbs (eds.), *Nova: 1965-1975*, London: Pavilion Books, 1993.

5 Michel Houellebecq, *Whatever*, London: Serpent's Tail, 1998, p. 99.

6 George Saunders, 'The 400-Pound CEO' in *CivilWarLand in Bad Decline*, London: Vintage, 1997, p. 63.

LIBERATING THE BILLBOARD?

1 John Hegarty, foreword in David Bernstein, *Advertising Outdoors: Watch this Space!*, London and New York: Phaidon, 2004 (first published 1997), p. 5.

2 David Ogilvy, *Confessions of an Advertising Man*, New York: Atheneum, 1963, p. 127.

3 See Kate Linker, *Love for Sale: The Words and Pictures of Barbara Kruger*, New York: Abrams, 1990, and Ann Goldstein et al., *Barbara Kruger*, Los Angeles: Museum of Contemporary Art, 1999.

LOYALTY BEYOND REASON

1 Kevin Roberts, *Lovemarks: The Future beyond Brands*, New York: PowerHouse Books, 2004, p. 22.

2 http://www.lovemarks.com

3 *Lovemarks*, p. 152.

4 Ibid., p. 50.

A WORLD WITHOUT ADS

1 Jim Heimann (ed.), *All-American Ads of the 40s*, Cologne: Taschen, 2001 and *All-American Ads of the 50s*, Cologne: Taschen, 2001.

2 Vance Packard, *The Hidden Persuaders*, Penguin Books, new edition, 1981 (first published 1957).

3 Raymond Hawkey, 'Advertising: The Skeleton in the Consumer's Cupboard', *Ark*, no. 5, 1952, p. 8.

4 The British design organization D&AD introduced an 'integrated creativity' category into its annual design awards in 2003.

LOOK AT MY SPEECHTOOL

1 http://www.trashbat.co.ck

THE CITIZEN DESIGNER

1 Milton Glaser, 'This is What I Have Learned', conference paper presented at 'Voice2: AIGA National Design Conference', Washington, March 2002, http://voiceconference.aiga.org/transcripts/presentations/milton_glaser.pdf

2 Samina Quraeshi, 'The Architecture of Change', conference paper presented at 'Voice2: AIGA National Design Conference, Washington, March 2002, http://voiceconference.aiga.org/transcripts/presentations/samina_quraeshi.pdf

3 Sheri Koetting, 'Voice Essays', AIGA website, 2002, http://voiceconference.aiga.org/voiceessays.html

4 'The Architecture of Change'.

5 Bennett Peji, 'Voice Essays', AIGA website, 2002, http://voiceconference.aiga.org/voiceessays.html

6 Ibid.

7 'This is What I Have Learned'.

RAMSHACKLE UTOPIAS

1 Simon Midgley, 'Finding the Plot', *Guardian*, 4 April 2000.

2 Select Committee on the Environment, Transport and Regional Affairs, fifth report, *The Future of Allotments*, 24 June 1998.

3 Claude Lévi-Strauss, *The Savage Mind*, Oxford University Press, 1996 (first published 1962).

4 Quoted in 'Finding the Plot'.

5 Quoted in *The Future of Allotments*.

6 Department of the Environment, Transport and the Regions, The Government's Response to the Environment, Transport and Regional Affairs Committee's Report, *The Future of Allotments*, 13 November 1998.

NEW EUROPE, NEW SPIRIT?

1 Iva Janáková, 'Graphic Design of the 1990s' in Typo Design Club, no. 3, Prague: *Typo Design Club 2000*, 1999, p. 6.

2 Iva Janáková et al., *Ladislav Sutnar – Prague – New York – Design in Action*, Prague: Museum of Decorative Arts and Argo Publishers, 2003.

3 Dejan Kršić, 'Fiasco Follows Form' in *Croatian Design Annual*, no. 2, Zagreb: Croatian Designers' Society, 2001, pp. 14-15.

4 Ibid., p. 12.

5 Quoted in Clare Dowdy, 'Poster Child', *Print*, LVII:IV, July/August 2003, p. 71.

6 Lana Cavar, 'Croatian Design', Icograda website, undated (c. 2002), http://www.icograda.org//web/feature-past-single.shtml?pfl=feature-single-2.param&op2.rfi=157

7 'Poster Child', p. 73.

WRITING WITH PICTURES

1 Robin Kinross, 'Judging a Book by its Material Embodiment: A German-English Example' in *Unjustified Texts*, London: Hyphen Press, 2002, pp. 186-99.

2 Maya Jaggi, 'Recovered Memories', *Guardian*, 22 September 2001.

3 Eric Homberger, 'W.G. Sebald', *Guardian*, 17 December 2001.

4 W.G. Sebald, *Austerlitz*, London: Penguin Books, 2002, pp. 275-6.

5 Ibid., pp. 268, 272.

6 Ibid., p. 281.

TECHNOLOGY IN EVERYDAY LIFE

1 The 'Making the Modern World' exhibition space was designed by Wilkinson Eyre Architects and the exhibition graphics are by Farrow Design. The project's director and lead curator was Andrew Nahum.

2 John Chris Jones, 'Softecnica' in John Thackara (ed.), *Design after Modernism: Beyond the Object*, London: Thames & Hudson, 1988, p. 216.

3 Timothy Boon, 'The Opportunities of Hybridity: *Making the Modern World*, a New Historical Gallery in a Diverse Institution', conference paper presented at 'Science Communication, Education, and the History of Science', Royal Society, London, July 2000, http://www.bshs.org.uk/conf/2000sciencecomm/papers/boon.doc

4 Ibid.

LOOK INWARD, AUSTRALIA

1 See Garry Emery, *Outside Inside Out/Inside Outside In*, Mulgrave: Images Publishing, 2002.

2 Geoffrey Caban, *A Fine Line: A History of Australian Commercial Art*, Sydney: Hale & Iremonger, 1983.

3 Ibid., p. 102.

4 Mimmo Cozzolino and Fysh Rutherford, *Symbols of Australia*, Melbourne: Mimmo Cozzolino, 2001 (first published 1980). See Jason Grant, 'Symbols of Assimilation', *Eye*, no. 56 vol. 14, summer 2005, pp. 38-9.

5 See *Ken Done: The Art of Design*, Sydney: Powerhouse Publishing, 1994.

6 David J. Tacey, *Edge of the Sacred: Transformation in Australia*, Melbourne: HarperCollins, 1998.

STRUGGLING TO BE HEARD

1 Robyn McDonald and Jason Grant, 'Introduction' in *Public x Private: Inkahoots 1990-2000*, Brisbane: Inkahoots (self-published), 2000.

2 Ross Fitzgerald, *A History of Queensland: From 1915 to the 1980s*, St Lucia: University of Queensland Press, 1984, p. 244.

3 There is an extensive literature on the subject. See Julie Ewington, 'Political Postering' in Paul Taylor (ed.), *Anything Goes: Art in Australia 1970-1980*, South Yarra: Art & Text, 1984; Lee-Anne Hall, *Who is Bill Posters? An Examination of Six Australian Socially Concerned Alternative Print Media Organisations*, Caper, no. 27, Australia Council, 1988; Clare Williamson, *Signs of the Times: Political Posters* in Queensland, Brisbane: Queensland Art Gallery, 1991; and Roger Butler, *Poster Art in Australia*, Canberra: National Gallery of Australia, 1993.

4 Neville Brody and Stuart Ewen, 'Design Insurgency', *Print*, XLIV:I, January/February 1990, p. 119.

5 Inkahoots' clients include: Brisbane City Council, Brisbane Urban Renewal, Ecological Engineering, Social Action Office, Queensland Conservation Council, Legal Aid Queensland, Relationships Australia, Family Planning Queensland, Australian Association of Young People in Care, Domestic Violence Resource Centre, Department of Youth Affairs, Prisoners' Legal Service, Anti-Discrimination Commission, Arts Queensland, Queensland Community Arts Network, La Boite Theatre, Queensland Poetry Festival, Queensland Writers' Centre, Brisbane Independent Filmmakers, Australians for Native Title and Reconciliation.

6 Jason Grant, 'Polite Obscenities' in *Public x Private*.

7 Ibid.

TASTE-FREE ZONE

1 *Mambo: Art Irritates Life*, Sydney: Mambo Graphics, 1994, p. 99. See also *Mambo: Still Life with Franchise*, Sydney: Mambo Graphics, 1998.

2 Ibid.

DESIGNING PORNOTOPIA

1 Andrea Dworkin, *Pornography: Men Possessing Women*, London: Women's Press, 1981, p. 224.

2 Ibid., p. 304.

3 Patrick Burgoyne, foreword in *Eboy Hello*, London: Laurence King Publishing, 2002.

4 Linda Williams, *Hard Core: Power, Pleasure, and the 'Frenzy of the Visible'*, London: Pandora Press, 1991, pp. 22-3.

COLLAPSING BULKHEADS

1 Will Self, *Junk Mail*, London: Bloomsbury, 1995,

pp. 340-1.

2 Quoted in Peter Ronnov-Jessen, 'Against Entropy', *The Literary Review*, August 1984, p. 31.

3 J.G. Ballard, *Crash*, London: Vintage, 2004, p. 9.

4 J.G. Ballard, *A User's Guide to the Millennium: Essays and Reviews*, London: HarperCollins, 1996. p. 84.

5 J.G. Ballard, 'Introduction to the French Edition of *Crash* (1974)' in *Crash*, London: Triad/Panther, 1985, p. 9. A shorter version of the introduction can be found in *Crash*, London: Vintage, 2004.

6 *Crash*, 2004, p. 44.

7 *Crash*, 1985, p. 8.

8 Mark Dery, 'Sex Drive', *21.C*, no. 4, 1997, p. 47.

THE SEX DETECTIVES

1 Tom Hingston et al., *Porn?*, London: Vision On, 2002.

BARING IT ALL

1 Peter Hall, *Sagmeister: Made You Look*, London: Booth-Clibborn Editions, 2001.

2 Ibid., p. 65.

3 Ibid., p. 32.

4 See Malcolm Green (ed.), *Brus, Muehl, Nitsch, Schwarzkogler: Writings of the Vienna Actionists*, London: Atlas Press, 1999.

5 *Sagmeister: Made You Look*, p. 279.

6 Robin Kinross in *Karel Martens: Printed Matter/Drukwerk*, London: Hyphen Press, 1996, p. 23.

7 Bob Gill, *Forget All the Rules about Graphic Design. Including the Ones in this Book*, New York: Watson-Guptill Publications, 1985 (first published 1981).

8 Ibid.

9 Katherine McCoy, 'Countering the Tradition of the Apolitical Designer' (1993) in Robyn Marsack (ed.), *Essays on Design 1: AGI's Designers of Influence*, London: Booth-Clibborn Editions, 1997, p. 90.

10 *Sagmeister: Made You Look*, p. 276.

11 Ibid., p. 237.

12 Stefan Sagmeister, 'Tweedledee, Tweedledum', *Communication Arts*, Design Annual, 2001, p. 248.

13 Ibid., p. 246.

14 Ibid., p. 252.

THE SKIN CULT

1 V. Vale and Andrea Juno (eds) *Re/Search*, no. 12, *Modern Primitives*, San Francisco: Re/Search Publications, 1989.

FLESH SPEAKS

1 Danzig Baldaev et al., *Russian Criminal Tattoo Encyclopaedia*, London: Steidl/Fuel, 2003.

2 Ibid., p. 51.

CYBER BJÖRK

1 Quoted in Barry Miles, *Bowie in His Own Words*, London: Omnibus Press, 1980, p. 26.

2 Quoted in Donald McQuade and Christine McQuade, *Seeing & Writing*, Boston and New York: Bedford/St Martin's, 2000, p. 432.

3 Quoted in Stuart Bailie, interview with Björk, *New Musical Express*, 3 October 1998.

4 Neil Tennant, foreword in Philip Hoare, *Icons of Pop*, London: Booth-Clibborn Editions/National Portrait Gallery, 1999, p. 4.

5 'Björk vs Me Company', *Idea*, no. 273, March 1999.

6 Donna J. Haraway, 'A Cyborg Manifesto' in *Simians, Cyborgs, and Women: The Reinvention of Nature*, London: Free Association Books, 1991, p. 180.

FOLLOW YOUR BLISS

1 Dick Hebdige, 'Postscript 4: Learning to Live on the Road to Nowhere' in *Hiding in the Light: On Images and Things*, London: Routledge, 1988.

2 Elliott Earls, 'Philosophy' in Cranbrook Academy of Art prospectus, 2002, p. 57.

3 Ibid.

APPLY FOR AN UPGRADE TODAY

1 *Nip/Tuck*, series 1, episode 3, Warner Bros., 2003.

2 Ibid.

3 Quoted in Angelika Taschen (ed.), *Aesthetic Surgery*, Cologne: Taschen, 2005, pp. 224, 258 and 249.

4 Ibid., p. 188.

5 Ibid., p. 198.

6 Ibid., p. 185.

7 *Top Santé*, September 2005, pp. 49-55.

8 Gregory Stock, *Redesigning Humans: Choosing our Children's Genes*, London: Profile Books, 2002.

9 *Aesthetic Surgery*, p. 256.

10 Quoted in Brian Alexander, 'Don't Die, Stay Pretty', *Wired*, no. 8.01, January 2000, http://www.wired.com/wired/archive/8.01/forever.html?pg=1&topic=&topic_set=

11 Natasha Vita-More, 'Radical Body Design "Primo 3M+"', 2002, http://www.kurzweilai.net/meme/frame.html?main=/articles/art0405.html

12 Anthony Dunne and Fiona Raby, *Consuming Monsters: Big, Perfect, Infectious*, London: self-published, 2003, p. 2.

13 Ibid., p. 4.

WHAT'S THE MATTER WITH US?

1 Paul Davis, *God Knows*, London: Browns, 2004.

2 Paul Davis, *Blame Everyone Else*, London: Browns, 2003.

3 Paul Davis, *Us & Them*, London: Laurence King Publishing, 2004.

4 Paul Davis, *Lovely*, Paris: Collette, 2003.

INDEX

CREDITS & THANKS

PICTURE CREDITS

p. 13. Photograph courtesy of the Office for Metropolitan Architecture.
pp. 33, 40, 99, 102. Fredrika Lökholm +44(0)7815 777 278.
p. 58. www.adbusters.org
p. 79. © Malcolm Garrett.
p. 173. Courtesy of One Little Indian Records.

I would like to thank the following publications, where earlier versions of these essays first appeared, sometimes under different titles. 'Hyphenation Nation' was published in 2002 in *Harvard Design Magazine*. 'Meet Me at the Checkout' appeared in the *Financial Times*. 'Luxurious Frugality', 'What do Men Want?', 'Loyalty beyond Reason', 'Look at My Speechtool', 'Mr Hancock's New Wave Art Class', 'Look Inward, Australia', 'Struggling to be Heard', 'Collapsing Bulkheads', 'The Sex Detectives', 'Flesh Speaks', 'Follow Your Bliss' and 'What's the Matter with Us?' appeared in *Eye* or on its website. 'A World without Ads', 'Taste-Free Zone', 'Designing Pornotopia' and 'The Skin Cult' appeared in *Print*. 'The Citizen Designer' appeared in *Trace*. 'Apply for an Upgrade Today' appeared in *I.D.* 'This Month's Cover' was published, in French, in *In Media Res: Information, Contre-Information*, Presses Universitaires de Rennes, 2003. 'Liberating the Billboard?' was published, in French, in *Art Grandeur Nature 2004*, Synesthésie Éditions, 2004. 'Ramshackle Utopias' was published in *Impossible Worlds: The Architecture of Perfection*, August/Birkhäuser, 2000. 'Baring it All' was published in *Stefan Sagmeister: Handarbeit*, MAK, 2002. 'Cyber Björk' was published in *Björk*, Little-i, 2001. 'New Europe, New Spirit?' was presented as a lecture at an ATypI conference in Prague, September 2004. Parts of 'Writing with Pictures' were presented as a lecture at a GraficEurope conference in Berlin, October 2004, and on the weblog *Design Observer*. 'Technology in Everyday Life' and the introduction were written for the book.

My thanks to the following editors: William S. Saunders at *Harvard Design Magazine*, Julia Cuthbertson at the *Financial Times*, Alice Twemlow, formerly at *Trace* (published by AIGA) and at GraficEurope, Julie Lasky at *I.D.*, Morten Salling at Art Grandeur Nature, and Nick Barley and Stephen Coates at August. Thanks to Alan Zaruba in Prague and to Tim Marshall and the University of Western Sydney for making the Australian research possible. I am hugely grateful to John L. Walters at *Eye* and to Joyce Rutter Kaye at *Print* for the tremendous support they have shown by publishing regular columns as well as other writing.

Much appreciation to the team that worked on this book: Jo Lightfoot, Donald Dinwiddie and Andy Prince at Laurence King Publishing and Nick Bell and Ken Leung at Nick Bell design.

208